The Heavenly Power of Divine Obedience and Gratitude

Part 1

The Heavenly Power of Divine Obedience and Gratitude

Part 1

Spiritual Discourses of
Shaykh Muhammad Hisham Kabbani

PUBLISHED BY THE
INSTITUTE FOR SPIRITUAL AND CULTURAL ADVANCEMENT

Published and Distributed by:

Institute for Spiritual and Cultural Advancement (ISCA)
17195 Silver Parkway, #201
Fenton, MI 48430 USA
Tel: (888) 278-6624
Fax: (810) 815-0518
Email: staff@naqshbandi.org
Web: http://www.naqshbandi.org

Second Edition: January 2013
THE HEAVENLY POWER OF DIVINE OBEDIENCE AND GRATITUDE, PART 1
ISBN: 978-1-930409-86-6

Library of Congress Cataloging-in-Publication Data

Kabbani, Muḥammad Hisham.
Spiritual discourses of Shaykh Muḥammad Hisham Kabbani.—1st ed.
p. cm.—(The heavenly power of divine obedience and gratitude, part 1)
Includes bibliographical references.
ISBN 978-1-930409-86-6 (alk. paper)
1. Naqshabandiyah. 2. Sufism. I. Title.
BP189.7.N352K327 2010
297.4'8—dc22
2010044186

PRINTED IN THE UNITED STATES OF AMERICA
15 14 13 12 11 05 06 07 08 09

Mawlana Shaykh Hisham Kabbani presents *Ramaḍān Series 2011* in the renowned Naqshbandi *zawiya* in Michigan. Since 1999, the shaykh has observed the age-old tradition of shaykhs of the famed Naqshbandi Golden Chain by performing the night prayers and *awrad* in congregation before sunrise, followed by a spiritual discourse throughout the holy month of Ramaḍān. This popular program has been broadcast on Sufilive.com since 2005 and reaches tens of thousands of viewers worldwide. This book is based on those discourses. (August 2011)

Table of Contents

About the Author i
Preface iii
Publisher's Notes v
Masters of the Naqshbandi-Haqqani Golden Chain ix
Recitation before Every Association 1
Your Reality Is Outside the Box 1
- The Mirror and the Image 2
- The Value of Steadfastness 4
- The Real Guides 5

The Heavenly Power of Reciting "RabbunAllah" 9
- Thank Allah! 9
- The Virtue of Living a Simple Life 10
- The Keys of Your Code to All Knowledge 13

Know Who Is Written as Your Shaykh 17
- The Childish Ego 17
- The Genuine Shaykh Versus a Plastic Shaykh 21

Imam al-Ghazali on Doubt and Submission 25
- The Battle Between Doubt and Obedience 25
- Total Compliance Raises You 26
- Strong Belief and Love Lead to Submission 28

Attributes of the Real Murshid 33
- Be the Blacksmith or the Perfumer 34
- Power to Remove the Negative and Instill the Positive 36
- Signs of a True Murshid 37

Trustees of the Divine Secrets 39
- Who Are the Trustees? 40
- The Darkness of Complaining 42

The Heavenly Benefits of Following a True Murshid 45
- Meditation Will Raise Your Station 46
- Five Benefits of the Relationship with a True Murshid 48
- Reality and Its Image 49

The Best Miracle Is to Be Consistent 51
- How to Fight Fatigue 52
- Seek the Heavenly Sustenance 53
- Love of Awliya Reflects Love of Allah and His Prophet 55

The Company of Saints Brings Righteousness 59
- Granted Knowledge Versus Learned Knowledge 59
- Those Who Mirror the Pious 61
- When Love of Goodness Takes Root, It Can't Be Cut 64

Journey to the Heavenly Presence through Rabitah 65
- Fragrance of the Pious Is Everywhere 65
- Benefit from Keeping the Shaykh's Company 66
- The Ka'bah within Your Heart 68

The Secret Treasure of "Obey Allah" 71
Safety and Fulfillment through Its Recitation 72
Street Markets Are Diversions of This World 73
Surrender, Avoid Fitna and Make Your Shaykh Happy 75
Awliyaullah Monitor Our Reactions 77
How the Sahabah Spread the Light of Islam 77
The Grant of Heavenly Knowledge and Your Amanat 79
Patience and Thankfulness, the Two Halves of Faith 85
Who Will Sit on the Heavenly Throne? 86
Three Elements of Knowledge: Islam, Iman and Ihsan 88
Be Patient, Make Peace and Forgive 88
The Power of Presenting Our Dhikr to Shah Naqshband 93
The Challenge of Sayyidina Bayazid al-Bistami 95
The Holy Ascension Is Continuous and Impacts Us 96
Allah's Words and Their Secrets Never End 98
Patience During Affliction Is Essential 101
Surety that Allah Rewards Tenfold 102
Reach Realities with Discipline and Obedience 104
The Believer Is the Mirror of His Brother 107
How Veils Are Lifted in Naqshbandi Tariqah 107
Why You Need a Mirror 109
Removing the Obstacle of Doubt 111
Divine Miracles and Mercy through the Awliya 113
Sayyidina 'Abdul Khaliq al-Ghujdawani 113
The Happy Angels and Power of Abi Zamzam 116
Secrets of Laylat al-Bara'ah 117
Sayyidina Shah Naqshband 123
Sayyīdinā Bayazid al-Bistami 126
Sayyidina Qasim bin Muhammad bin Abu Bakr 127
Islamic Calendar and Holy Days 133
Glossary 137
Other Publications 143

About the Author

Shaykh Kabbani is a renowned religious scholar of both traditional Islamic law and the spiritual science of Sufism. He hails from a respected family of traditional Islamic scholars, which includes the former head of the Association of Muslim Scholars of Lebanon and the present Grand Mufti (highest Islamic religious authority) of Lebanon.

For three decades he has promoted traditional Islamic principles of peace, love, compassion and social cohesion, while rigorously opposing extremism. As deputy leader of the Naqshbandi Haqqani Sufi Order, he is authorized to issue religious edicts and counsel students of the movement, which by recent reports number in the millions.

Since the early 1990s, Shaykh Kabbani has been pivotal in helping non-Muslim societies understand the difference between moderate mainstream Muslims and minority extremist sects.

In 2010, the shaykh hosted HRH Prince Charles of Wales. He has hosted two international conferences in the U.S. and various regional conferences around the world. His counsel is sought by journalists, academics, policymakers, community leaders and activists.

In the United States, Shaykh Kabbani serves as Chairman, Islamic Supreme Council of America; Founder, Naqshbandi Sufi Order of America; Advisor, World Organization for Resource Development and Education; and Chairman, As-Sunnah Foundation of America. In the United Kingdom, Shaykh Kabbani founded the Centre for Spiritual and Cultural Advancement and is lead scholar for the Sufi Muslim Council, a non-profit NGO that consults to the British government on public policy and social and religious issues. He has launched popular websites, such as eShaykh.com, SufiLive.com, spiritandculture.org.uk and islamicsupremecouncil.org.

Shaykh Kabbani has written numerous books on Islamic spirituality. He is well known in policy development circles and has presented several critical position papers on the current state of global Islam, counter-terrorism, and the primacy of democratic principles in Islam. In 2011, the shaykh issued an unprecedented *fatwa, The Prohibition of Domestic Violence in Islam,* (ISBN 9781930409972) which cites Islamic texts that condemn family violence.

Other titles by Shaykh Kabbani include: *The Sufilive Series* (2010-2012, 6 vols.), *At the Feet of My Master* (2010, 2 vols.), *The Nine-fold Ascent* (2009), *Banquet for the Soul* (2008), *Illuminations* (2007), *Universe Rising* (2007), *Symphony of Remembrance* (2007), *A Spiritual Commentary on the Chapter of Sincerity* (2006), *The Sufi Science of Self-Realization* (Fons Vitae, 2005), *Keys to the Divine Kingdom* (2005), *Classical Islam and the Naqshbandi Sufi Order* (2004), *The Naqshbandi Sufi Tradition Guidebook* (2004), *The Approach of Armageddon? An Islamic Perspective* (2003), *Encyclopedia of Muḥammad's Women Companions and the Traditions They Related* (1998, with Dr. Laleh Bakhtiar), *Encyclopedia of Islamic Doctrine* (7 vols. 1998), *Angels Unveiled* (1996), *The Naqshbandi Sufi Way* (1995), and *Remembrance of God Liturgy of the Sufi Naqshbandi Masters* (1994).

Preface

This book is based on the *suḥbah,* extemporaneous, divinely inspired discourses, of Shaykh Hisham Kabbani, disciple and representative of the global head of the Naqshbandi-Haqqani Sufi Order, Mawlana Shaykh Nazim Adil al-Haqqani. Their uplifting discourses often include anecdotes of venerable Sufi masters from the renowned Naqshbandi Golden Chain, which dates back to Prophet Muḥammad ﷺ.

The Heavenly Power of Divine Obedience and Gratitude, Volume 1 features many insightful quotations from illustrious shaykhs throughout history. These particular discourses were featured in the author's highly coveted "Ramaḍān Series" of 2011. In the holy month of Ramaḍān, attendees arrive at the shaykh's humble *zawiya* in pre-dawn hours, where they observe special spiritual practices and prayers followed by his discourse, which is broadcast daily around the world to an eager audience.

One need not be a current traveler on the Sufi Path to benefit from the lessons in this book, which may help you acquire your unique 'code' to unlock spiritual knowledge, learn energizing practices that eliminate fatigue, or achieve that elusive state of inner-self/outer-world balance. These lessons are the antidote for internal chaos and can help restore your connection to heavenly power.

For fifty years, the author has sought to serve his master and promote these ancient Sufi teachings in the best manner. We hope this book reflects this spirit and opens a beautiful, inviting door to *The Heavenly Power of Divine Obedience and Gratitude.*

Publisher's Notes

This book is directed to those familiar with the Sufi Way; however, to accommodate lay readers unfamiliar with Sufi terminology and practices, we have provided English translations of Arabic texts and a comprehensive glossary. Where Arabic terms are crucial to the discussion, we have included transliteration and explanations. For readers familiar with Arabic and Islamic teachings, for further clarity please consult the cited sources.

The original material is based on transcripts of a series of holy gatherings known as *ṣuḥbah*, a divinely inspired talk given by the "shaykh," a highly trained spiritual guide. To present the authentic flavor of such rare teachings, great care was taken to preserve the speaking styles of both the author and the illustrious shaykhs upon whose notes this book is based.

Translations from Arabic to English pose unique challenges that we have tried our best to make understandable to Western readers. Please note our application of the common Arabic oral tradition of omitting definite articles such as "~~the~~ Prophet" and "~~the~~ Holy Qur'an," as practiced by Muslims around the world as intimate references.

We apply contemporary American English publishing standards and therefore do not italicize commonly known foreign nouns (jihād, Qur'an, shaykh) unless they appear in transliterations.

Quotes from the Holy Qur'an and Holy Traditions of Prophet Muḥammad are offset, italicized and cited.

The pronoun "they" is frequently used by Sufi guides to reference heavenly beings and holy souls who support them and give them orders, a usage that appears throughout this book. Where gender-specific pronouns such as "he" and "him" are applied in a general sense, no discrimination is intended towards women, upon whom The Almighty bestowed great honor.

Islamic teachings are primarily based on four sources, in this order:

- **Holy Qur'an**: the Islamic holy book of divine revelation (God's Word) granted to Prophet Muḥammad. Reference to Holy Qur'an appears as "4:12," which indicates "Chapter 4, Verse 12."
- **Sunnah**: holy traditions of Prophet Muḥammad ﷺ; the systematic recording of his words and actions that comprise the *ḥadīth*. For fifteen centuries, Islam has applied a strict, highly technical standard, rating

each narration in terms of its authenticity and categorizing its "transmission." As this book is not highly technical, we simplified the reporting of *ḥadīth,* but included the narrator and source texts to support the discussion at hand.

- ***Ijma*ʿ:** The adherence, or agreement of the experts of independent reasoning *(āhl al-ijtihād)* to the conclusions of a given ruling pertaining to what is permitted and what is forbidden after the passing of the Prophet, Peace be upon him, as well as the agreement of the Community of Muslims concerning what is obligatorily known of the religion with its decisive proofs. Perhaps a clearer statement of this principle is, "We do not separate (in belief and practice) from the largest group of the Muslims."
- **Legal Rulings:** highly trained Islamic scholars form legal rulings from their interpretation of the Qur'an and the Sunnah, known as *ijtihād.* Such rulings are intended to provide Muslims an Islamic context regarding contemporary social norms. In theological terms, scholars who form legal opinions have completed many years of rigorous training and possess degrees similar to a doctorate in divinity in Islamic knowledge, or in legal terms, hold the status of a high court or supreme court judge, or higher.

The following universally recognized symbols have been respectfully included in this work. While they may seem tedious, they are deeply appreciated by a vast majority of our readers.

ﷻ *Subḥānahu wa Taʿalā* (may His Glory be Exalted), recited after the name "Allāh" and any of the Islamic names of God.

ﷺ *ṢallAllāhu ʿalayhi wa sallam* (God's blessings and greetings of peace be upon him), recited after the holy name of Prophet Muḥammad.

عليه السلام *ʿAlayhi ʿs-salām* (peace be upon him/her), recited after holy names of other prophets, names of Prophet Muḥammad's relatives, the pure and virtuous women in Islam, and angels.

رضي الله عنه/رضي الله عنها *RaḍīAllāhu ʿanh(um)* (may God be pleased with him/her), recited after the holy names of Companions of Prophet Muḥammad; plural: *raḍīAllāhu ʿanhum.*

ق represents *QaddasAllāhu sirrah* (may God sanctify his secret), recited after names of saints.

Transliteration

Transliteration from Arabic to English poses challenges. To show respect, Muslims often capitalize nouns which, in English, appear in lowercase.

To facilitate authentic pronunciation of names, places and terms, use the following key:

Symbol	**Transliteration**	**Symbol**	**Transliteration**	**Vowels: Long**	
ء	‘	ط	ţ	آ ى	**ā**
ب	b	ظ	Ɛ	و	**ū**
ت	t	ع	¿	ي	**ī**
ث	th	غ	gh	**Short**	
ج	j	ف	f	َ	**a**
ح	ħ	ق	q	ُ	**u**
خ	kh	ك	k	ِ	**i**
د	d	ل	l		
ذ	dh	م	m		
ر	r	ن	n		
ز	z	ه	h		
س	s	و	w		
ش	sh	ي	y		
ص	š	ة	ah; at		
ض	ļ	ال	**al-/’l-**		

Masters of the Naqshbandi-Haqqani Golden Chain

May Allāh ﷻ preserve their secrets.

1. Prophet Muḥammad ibn ʿAbdAllāh ﷺ
2. Abū Bakr as-Ṣiddīq ق
3. Salmān al-Farsi ق
4. Qasim bin Muḥammad bin Abū Bakr ق
5. Jafar aṣ-Ṣādiq ق
6. Tayfur Abū Yazīd al-Bistāmi ق
7. AbūlHassan ʿAlī al-Kharqani ق
8. Abū ʿAlī al-Farmadi ق
9. Abū Yaqūb Yusūf al-Hamadani ق
10. AbūlAbbas, al-Khiḍr ق
11. ʿAbdul Khāliq al-Ghujdawani ق
12. Arif ar-Riwakri ق
13. Khwaja Maḥmūd al-Anjir al-Faghnawi ق
14. ʿAlī ar-Ramitani ق
15. Muḥammad Baba as-Samasi ق
16. as-Sayyid Amir Kulal ق
17. Muḥammad Bahaʿuddin Shah Naqshband ق
18. Alaʿuddin al-Bukhāri al-Attar ق
19. Yaqūb al-Charkhi ق
20. Ubaydullāh al-Ahrar ق
21. Muḥammad az-Zahid ق
22. Darwish Muḥammad ق
23. Muḥammad Khwaja al-Amkanaki ق
24. Muḥammad al-Baqi billāh ق
25. Aḥmad al-Farūqi as-Sirhindi ق
26. Muḥammad al-Masum ق
27. Muḥammad Sayfuddin al-Farūqi al-Mujaddidi ق
28. as-Sayyid Nūr Muḥammad al-Badawani ق
29. Shamsuddin Habib Allāh ق
30. ʿAbdAllāh ad-Dahlawi ق
31. Khālid al-Baghdādī ق
32. Ismail Muḥammad ash-Shirwāni ق
33. Khas Muḥammad Shirwāni ق
34. Muḥammad Effendi al-Yaraghi ق
35. Jamāluddin al-Ghumuqi al-Ḥusayni ق
36. Abū Aḥmad as-Sughuri ق
37. Abū Muḥammad al-Madani ق
38. Sharafuddīn ad-Daghestāni ق
39. ʿAbdAllāh al-Faʿiz ad-Daghestāni
40. Muḥammad Nazim Adil al-Haqqani ق

1

Recitation before Every Association

بسم الله الرحمن الرحيم

A'ūdhu billāhi min ash-Shayṭān ir-rajīm.
Bismillāhi' r-Raḥmāni 'r-Raḥīm.
Nawaytu 'l-arbā'īn, nawaytu 'l-'itikāf,
nawaytu'l-khalwah, nawaytu 'l-'uzlah,
nawaytu 'r-riyāḍa, nawaytu 's-sulūk,
lillāhi Ta'alā fī hādhā 'l-masjid.

Atī'ūllāha wa atī' ūr-Rasūla
wa ūli'l-amri minkum.

I seek refuge in Allāh from Satan, the rejected.
In the Name of Allāh, the Merciful,
the Compassionate.
I intend the forty (days of seclusion);
I intend seclusion in the mosque,
I intend seclusion, I intend isolation,
I intend discipline (of the ego); I intend to travel
in God's Path for the sake of God,
in this mosque.

Obey Allāh, obey the Prophet,
and obey those in authority among you.
Sūrat an-Nisa (The Women), 4:59

Your Reality Is Outside the Box

A'ūdhu billāhi min ash-Shayṭāni 'r-rajīm. Bismillāhi' r-Raḥmāni 'r-Raḥīm. Nawaytu 'l-arbā'īn, nawaytu 'l-'itikāf, nawaytu'l-khalwah, nawaytu 'l-'uzlah, nawaytu 'r-riyāḍa, nawaytu 's-sulūk, lillāhi Ta'alā fī hādhā 'l-masjid. Atī'ūllāha wa atī'ū 'r-Rasūla wa ūli 'l-amri minkum. (4:59)

K*alīmatān khafifatān 'alā al-lisān thaqīlatān fi'l-mīzaān. SubḥānAllāhi wa biḥamdihi subḥānAllāhi 'l-'Aẓīm astāghfirullāh.* With *shafā'a*, intercession of the Prophet ﷺ, we are asking Allāh ﷻ to forgive us. Allāh ﷻ said in the Holy Qur'an:

> *If they had (only) remained on the (right) Way, We should certainly have bestowed on them rain in abundance.* (Sūrat al-Jinn, 72:16)

It means, "If they would stand forth on the Path, We would shower them with heavy rain, and as rain comes heavily, We send them Our mercy; I make them angels, *awlīyāullāh*, and *aḥbābī*, My lovers."

People come from everywhere seeking Allāh's love and our *shuyūkh's* support; there is nothing else. They give up time with their children and families, and some bring their families with them. Allāh is The Merciful and He knows why everyone comes. No one comes for *dunya;* all are coming for *Ākhirah.*

Allāh ﷻ gave everyone something that He did not give the other, just as Allāh gave every prophet something He did not give the other, but He gave one more than He gave all others. If you add everything prophets received, it will not be a drop in the ocean of Sayyīdinā Muḥammad ﷺ! That is why in *jama'ah,* congregation, Allāh always gives something special, but there will be one whom even if you were to add all what the others get, they will not be a drop in his ocean.

An example of this is found in the lifecycle of bees: the queen is only one in the group and Allāh gave her a specialty that if there is no queen there is no honey, in fact there is nothing. Although every bee has something different from other bees, they can only make honey because of their queen, that one to whom Allāh gave more. That specialty is given only to one, there cannot be two as two cannot be on the same level; there can be two and three on the mercy that will be divided to them. However, there must be one queen attracting all other bees, and this is what we call the master or shaykh.

Lā bud min murshidīn hissī. There is no way but to have a *murshid* only spiritually, but you must see him; he must exist physically. You cannot say, "I connect with my teacher who is in the grave," because in the grave that connection is finished. You need someone *hissī*, a living shaykh, one who inherits from the Prophet ﷺ what his students need. Every student, every member of *ummat an-Nabī* ﷺ has a wire from his heart to Prophet's heart, and if that wire is disrupted somewhere, you will not get any flow of information: it must be from a direct connection with the Prophet ﷺ.

Don't think that is impossible. The Prophet ﷺ mentioned it in his *ḥadīth,* "I observe the *ʿāmal* of my nation." If there is no connection, how does he observe? With wireless technology they pull more from electromagnetic waves and through telepathy they can reach even more. That is why *awlīyāullāh* reach all their students, but those students cannot reach everyone. The shaykh has a wireless network and wherever he is, heavenly Wifi reaches him and through it he reaches the Prophet ﷺ and presents all the students. If human beings can reach with a Wifi, why can't a *walī* reach with a heavenly Wifi?

Wa kullun min Rasūlullāhi multamisan, "All of them are taking from the Prophet ﷺ." That means all *awlīyā*, all *anbīyā*, and all Creation must have a share to take something. Sometimes they have a cable or a big tube that houses thousands of small cables. It depends on the capacity of that *walī*, how many cables he can carry. A Sulṭān al-Awlīyā doesn't need cables as he reached heavenly manifestations and has heavenly Wifi through which he can always get information.

The Mirror and the Image

Allāh ﷻ said:

> *And of all things We have created pairs; perhaps you will remember.*
>
> (Sūrat al-Dhāriyāt, 51:49)

SubḥānAllāh. "From every thing We created two." Allāh ﷻ didn't say "one," He said "two." It's not male and female, forget about that; there is another *āyah* for that, but He said, "Of every thing We created two." We have two of him and two of him: we have one reality here (in this world) and one up, which means one reality and one image. So when *awlīyāullāh* want to see and know about your reality, they don't look at you here, because you are the image. It is like looking in a mirror: when you move right, the image moves left; when you move left, it moves right. So they don't look at the mirror to see your image, they don't look inside the box, they look outside the box. We are inside the box; when we go outside the box we find realities and when we go inside the box we find images.

So that is why Imām al-Ghazāli ؑ said, "When you die, then you will know your reality and be awake, and leave your image behind." The reality is outside *dunya*, the box, so when you leave *dunya* you reach reality. When *awlīyāullāh* look, as Grandshaykh and Mawlana Shaykh Nazim ق said, "Everyone has a reality, a star in this universe, whether big or small, depending on the reality of that person."

Allāh's will created realities and images that are like a shadow, and He ﷻ ordered them to follow the real form. With Allāh's wisdom and will, He ﷻ made the shadow move on its own through *irādatan juʿziyya*, a partial will, but He ﷻ left the real will with the reality that controls your nearness and presence in Allāh's Divine Presence.

Reality cannot be *tudannas*, it does not commit a sin or become dirty for it is pure and clean, always in Allāh's Presence glorifying Him. Allāh ﷻ has taught us how to glorify Him by the first chapter of the Holy Qur'an:

Alḥamdūlillāhi Rabbi'l-ʿAlāmīn.
Praise be to Allāh, the Lord of the Worlds. (Sūrat al-Fātiḥah, 1:1)

Allāh is glorifying Himself by Himself to Himself, saying, "*Alḥamdūlillāh.*" It means, "O My servant! Say '*alḥamdūlillāh!*'" In every moment our realities are saying "*alḥamdūlillāh*" in Allāh's Presence, and therefore, they are always clean.

That is why the Prophet ﷺ said:
Human beings are born on fitra, innocence; either his parents make him Jewish or Christian or Zoroastrian.

He didn't say, "His parents make him Muslim," because already Allāh ﷻ created him Muslim, clean. So it means the partial realities of his shadow move in different directions in his imaginary life. This is an imaginary life. Can anyone say, "I am not going to die," or, "will live forever." If so, show us your power: go to the graveyard and make everyone wake up! So the shadow acts in *dunya,* but the reality does not. So we need *murshidīn hissī,* a living guide who is real, not someone who calls himself *'murshid.'* It is not easy to become a *murshid;* it is only by Allāh ﷻ's grant and a *murshid* must meet certain specifications that do not come through their cleverness.

Lā bud min murshidīn hissī. You must have a physical *murshid* who will take all the wrong you committed in your shadow-form back to your reality, to make sure your reality is always glorifying Allāh ﷻ, saying, *"Alḥamdūlillāh."* When you say, *"Alḥamdūlillāh,"* Allāh is happy with you! That is why Sūrat al-Fātiḥah is read in every *raka'at* of prayer, as without reciting *"alḥamdūlillāh"* the prayer is not valid. You cannot begin reciting from *"Rabbi 'l-'Alāmīn"* with no *"alḥamdūlillāh;"* you must recite Sūrat al-Fātiḥah from beginning to end, which is all glorifying Allāh ﷻ.

The Value of Steadfastness

Stories narrated by Grandshaykh ق and Mawlana Shaykh, may Allāh grant him long life, are not fabricated; they really happened, because *awlīyāullāh* can see what is in the past, present, and future. They tell the story of a *walī* who never took showers and always sweated, and wherever he went his nice smell reached. One of his students had doubts, like many people today, and he said, "It is so strange that wherever he goes he has a nice smell. What kind of perfume is he using?" Then guidance came to his heart; Allāh opened his heart and he said, "Today I am going to make sure that I am present in the morning when my shaykh wakes up, and I will take him the pitcher of water for his *wudu* to see what he does."

They had no restrooms like today, so the shaykh went out to relieve himself in a field at the bottom of a cliff, away from people, and he returned after one minute. The *murīd* put water for his shaykh's *wudu* and he smelled a very beautiful fragrance coming from his shaykh, who said, "Come after me." The *murīd* didn't want to follow the shaykh, but he was curious to see what is there. The shaykh found three pieces of defecation and said, *"Mashā'Allāh!"* and put them in his turban.

The *murīd* thought, "What is this? Yesterday he ate a whole chicken and today he is making only three small drips with such a nice smell that never existed before!" Wherever the shaykh went, musk emanated from his turban. Although in Shari'ah that is not accepted, this is to tell us that the *murshid* is not the one who leaves a bad smell behind him, he only leaves a good smell. That is the *murshid* we need, and we must know Allāh ﷻ is Great and can provide us that!

Sayyīdinā ʿAbd al-Qādir Jilānī ق said to a 50-year-old man, "Know, O child!" It doesn't matter how old you are or if you have a short or long beard. "May Allāh favor you with the Straight Path, without which you are a child." For both men and women, if you want maturity and to carry responsibility, it means you must be on the Sirāt al-Mustaqīm, the Straight Path, or else you are still a child.

Prophet ﷺ said:

Know that the first step in Gnosticism is istiqāmah (steadfastness).

The scholars of my nation rank with the prophets of Bani Isrāʿīl.[1]

Without *istiqāmah* you will not get anything. This does not apply to common scholars who can be bought. Those are academic scholars whose knowledge is from papers. For knowledge of the heart there are only *awlīyāullāh,* whom the Prophet ﷺ described as "*ʿālīmūn ʿāmil,*" those who perform what they learn. So if you are on the Right Path, Allāh will make you a scholar that inherits from prophets.

The door to that level is *istiqāmah,* from which you cannot go astray; otherwise, you must repent and Allāh will forgive. We cannot claim we are *maʿsūm,* infallible, as only prophets are infallible. So since we are not *maʿsūm,* don't say a shaykh does not commit a sin as that is not true.

Sayyīdinā Ibrāhīm ﷺ is *maʿsūm* as he is a prophet. When the people asked him, "Who cut the necks of these idols?" he said, "I don't know," although he cut them, but he will not be judged for it. Sayyīdinā Yusūf's ﷺ brothers threw him in the well and they are all prophets; that was a big test for their father, Sayyīdinā Yaqūb ﷺ.

The Real Guides

So *awlīyā* are not *maʿsūm* as they sin, but they repent. Don't say, "That *walī* does not sin." He might sin, but his intention is good and he didn't mean it. That is Allāh's will, which must happen, so he has been set up by angels to fall and say to himself, "O self! You are dirty." Allāh makes His *awlīyāullāh* fall down to show them:

1 Narrated by Imam at-Tirmidhi in his book of *tafsīr* on the authority of ibn Saʿid al-Hakim; al-Bukhari in his Tarikh; at-Tabarani in his Kabir; Ibn ʿAdi in his Kamil, from Ibn ʿUmar.

Falā tuzakkū anfusakum.

Therefore, do not justify yourselves. (Sūrat al-Najm, 53:32)

"Don't glorify or praise yourself." Allāh ﷻ makes His saints fall into mistakes to remind them that they did something wrong in their life and repent for it. There is a big meaning here, something we have to taste. For example, when someone commits a sin, he tastes that sin and will regret it all his life. The root of *insān*, "Man," comes from *nisyān*, "forgetfulness." If *insān* doesn't forget his sins, all his life he will be depressed, so Allāh makes him forget. He repents and that bad deed is gone as Allāh forgives him and makes him forget.

A *walī* doesn't forget; if he is on the Straight Path and falls right or left, he continues to ask for forgiveness. We need such a guide; that is the guide we have to find as not everyone who claims they are a shaykh is a guide. Pharaoh proclaimed, "I am Your Lord, the Highest One!" but he forgot who he is.

Also, Allāh ﷻ said to Sayyīdinā ʿĪsā ﷺ:

O ʿĪsā, son of Maryam! Did you say to men, "Worship me and my mother as two gods besides Allāh?" He will say, "Glory be to You! It was not for me to say what I had no right. Had I said such a thing, You would surely have known it. You know what is in my inner self, though I do not know what is in Yours! Truly only You are the Knower of All that is Hidden and Unseen."

(Sūrat al-Ma'idah, 5:116)

Confirming to him, to make him feel the pressure of what others were saying, Allāh ﷻ asked, "*Yā* ʿĪsā! Did you tell the Apostles, 'Take me and my mother as two gods other than Allāh.'" Of course Allāh ﷻ knew the truth of the matter, but wanted to show Sayyīdinā ʿĪsā ﷺ, "You! Defend yourself!"

Sayyīdinā ʿĪsā ﷺ said, "If I said it You know it, as You know what is in my self, but I don't know what is in Your Self."

And then Allāh ﷻ said something to put him down further, "He and his mother ate food (used the toilet)." Allāh doesn't care if they are prophets or not as they are all His servants! It means, "How can people accept that you are a god and you use the toilet?" *Hāsha lillāh*!

When Allāh wants his *awlīyāullāh* to say something He sets them up, then they are pushed. "O, they made a mistake. Be careful and don't do it next time." *Tubna wa rajaʿna*, "We repent!" And so we need a guide at this level, not those who claim they are guides, as so many do. Pharaoh claimed, "I am Allāh!" Do we automatically accept that claim? If someone claims he is a shaykh, bring the proof!

We explained the four levels of *murshids* that Grandshaykh classified in detail. We recently published a book, *Who Are the Guides*?, that defines the four levels of shaykhs. Such guides carry the whole universe on their shoulders and say, "O our Lord! Give us more and we will carry it." They are not like the charlatans we see everywhere today.

May Allāh ﷻ forgive us and may Allāh ﷻ bless us.

Wa min Allāhi 't-tawfīq, bi ḥurmati 'l-ḥabīb, bi ḥurmati 'l-Fātiḥah.

And with Allāh is success. For the sake of the Beloved, for his sake we recite the opening chapter of Holy Qur'an.

The Heavenly Power of Reciting "RabbunAllah"

A'ūdhu billāhi min ash-Shayṭāni 'r-rajīm. Bismillāhi' r-Raḥmāni 'r-Raḥīm. Nawaytu 'l-arbā'īn, nawaytu 'l-'itikāf, nawaytu'l-khalwah, nawaytu 'l-'uzlah, nawaytu 'r-riyāḍa, nawaytu 's-sulūk, lillāhi Ta'alā fī hādhā 'l-masjid. Atī'ūllāha wa atī'ū 'r-Rasūla wa ūli 'l-amri minkum. (4:59)

Inshā-Allāh, we will go through and expand on some of what we have here regarding the Naqshbandi teachings and the blessings that Allāh ﷻ has sent on His Servant. First of all, let us put the foundation: *mā aḥad aḥsan min aḥad,* "No one is better than anyone else." Allāh ﷻ looks at everyone in Allāh's Way and we don't know: you might be the shaykh, the student or nothing, Allāh knows best. How many students were better than their shaykhs and yet Allāh gave them the power to reach the heart of human beings?

Alḥamdūlillāh, Allāh guided us and directed us to be at the threshold of Sayyīdinā Mawlana Shaykh Nazim al-Haqqani ق, who was on the threshold of his teacher, Grandshaykh 'AbdAllāh al-Fa'iz ad-Daghestāni ق. We were lucky to have spent some time with Grandshaykh and witness his relationship with Mawlana Shaykh, *alḥamdūlillāh,* from 1958 to 1973, when Grandshaykh left *dunya.* For fifteen years we accompanied two shaykhs and witnessed a lot of experiences in different ways from both. Although one followed the other, and this is the way from the time of the Prophet ﷺ up to al-Mahdi ؑ, we saw how they showed love to Allāh ﷻ, the Prophet ﷺ, *awlīyāullāh* and their students who were with them.

They were like rockets in their teaching, never exhausted from seeing *murīds* or from making *du'ā* for those who ask. Always they were on the Straight Path, Ṣirāt al-Mustaqīm, in such a way that, according to our knowledge and in everything we saw from them, daily there was something new that rendered us unable to record. They are the best example of teacher and student (very close and loving), such an example that made us always try to not be away from them.

Thank Allah!

I cannot say except *shukrānlillāh* and *alḥamdūlillāh. "Alḥamdūlillāh"* has a meaning and *"shukrānlillāh"* has a meaning and the two meanings have big differences. "*Alḥamdūlillāh*" is glorifying Allāh, as one of the meanings, and "*shukrānlillāh*" is thanking Allāh. You must say "*alḥamdūlillāh*" as it is the first word in Sūrat al-Fātiḥah. Therein, Allāh is praising Himself by Himself. But *shukrānlillāh* is from the *ʿabd* to His Lord. Allāh doesn't say "*shukrānlillāh,*" He says "*alḥamdūlillāh.*" Allāh didn't say, "*Shukrān* for Me," but we say *shukrān*.

Our Lord said:

Wa lā in shakartum la-azīdanakum.

If you thank Me, I will give you more. (Sūrat Ibrāhīm, 14:7)

So *shukr*, to give thanks, is an order to the servant to say every moment of his life, that Allāh is granting him a drink in this *dunya* and a drink in *Ākhirah*, where everyone will be thirsty. So in every moment you must say "*shukrānlillāh,*" and you must say "*alḥamdūlillāh,*" which is glorifying Allāh.

The Virtue of Living a Simple Life

I never saw Mawlana Shaykh or Grandshaykh complain. They both lived very simple lives, which is the theme of this year's Ramaḍān Series.

You need a *murshid*. Not everyone can say they are a *murshid*, as to give *irshād* (guidance) is one thing and to lecture and lead *dhikr* is something else. Guidance will put you on Ṣirāt al-Mustaqīm. *Awlīyāullāh* will carry their followers if they are handicapped, but Ṣirāt al-Mustaqīm is not cheap, it is expensive. The way these *shuyūkh* lived is like a Stone Age life, very primitive and simple, that to us is like a chicken coop but which for them is a palace! They don't look with the eyes of the head only, but they look with the eyes of their heart and see that chicken coop is a paradise.

To build the foundation of this series, I will describe Grandshaykh's house, comprised of two rooms and one kitchen. His bedroom and living room measure 15x12 feet. Between the two rooms is a small hallway and the door to the kitchen. The house is made from mud and is located on top of Mt. Qasiyoun in Damascus.

When it was built, it was the only house on the mountain, which is so steep that no car would take you up and you had to climb. When we came from Lebanon to visit, when we reached Damascus the car didn't go up what is known as "Talʿat al-Muhajireen, the Hill of Immigrants." It was a very fancy area below and very simple area up on the mountain. We walked from where the taxi stopped and climbed the mountain, taking sixty-to-ninety minutes depending on where the taxi dropped us.

He put the guests in his living room. At ʿAsr time it is often very hot inside, perhaps 50 Centigrade (120 Fahrenheit), with no air conditioner, only a fan. We went out with Grandshaykh, may Allāh bless him, and with Mawlana Shaykh, and sat on the roof of the house, where Grandshaykh gave his *irshād*. It was such that a child might fall down from there as it had no fence at the edge of the roof. We and other guests sat there and Mawlana drank tea after praying ʿAsr, and he gave *suḥbah* up to Maghrib, for two hours. All Damascus is below and you can see all the way to Masjid al-Amawi and the whole city.

Inside the house the kitchen had no refrigerator. In the old traditional way, there was a cabinet to store dried meat if they had it, and their food was primarily vegetables, olives, cheese, bread and yogurt. That is how they passed their lives. Outside the house is the independent *wudu* area and I know for sure that not one among you will go to it (from its rustic condition). So they lived a very simple life, waking one or two hours before Fajr to pray Tahajjud. Grandshaykh did his *awrād* on his bed.

In winter they heated the place with a rustic wood stove with a door and a broken exhaust pipe that carried only some exhaust out the window. We came to pray Tahajjud with him in the early morning and it was so cold that you felt chilled to the bone! We arrived 1.5 hours before Fajr and could not see because of smoke that filled the house.

Grandshaykh ق sat reciting, *"Allāh, Allāh, Allāh, Allāh;"* he was not here. When he did his *awrād,* you could not approach him as the *tajallī* was so majestic it would frighten a lion! That *tajallī* was under the Divine Name, "al-Jabbar." Grandshaykh was so powerful that he moved mountains; in his presence you felt a tsunami will take you! You could hear not only his voice, but an infinite number of voices reciting.

Grandshaykh, may Allāh grant him the highest level to be with the Prophet ﷺ, used to say that as soon as he opened a *suḥbah,* by order of the Prophet ﷺ all *jinn* and *awlīyāullāh* around the world must be present, listening to him. Such a shaykh you have, Grandshaykh ق! He said Allāh ﷻ gave them heavenly hearing to direct themselves from their places to that *suḥbat.* At that time, we didn't understand how but we believed it. Today Allāh shows you that ability through technology. With Twitter, millions of people can hear from east and west via *dunya* instruments. When *awlīyāullāh* say that, all who are under that *tajallī* open their headsets and listen to that lecture. Now everyone can listen, so why do we accept that ability via technology but not from *awlīyā*?

Grandshaykh ق said to tell you about Imām al-Bukhāri ق, who collected *aḥadīth* of the Prophet ﷺ, Saḥih al-Bukhāri. His *masjid* and adjacent school in Bukhara can easily hold six-thousand worshippers, and when he gave a lecture at least twenty-five thousand people attended as Allāh ﷻ stretched it. If Allāh wills, He can expand this *dunya* and pass it through the eye of a needle; can the needle object? So when Imām al-Bukhāri gave his lecture, everyone was able to hear as if they were sitting beside him. That is only for those mentioned in the *ḥadīth:*

> *My servant does not cease to approach Me through voluntary worship until I will love him. When I love him, I will become the ears with which he hears, the eyes with which he sees, the hand with which he acts, and the tongue with which he speaks.* (Ḥadīth Qudsī)

With heavenly hearing, you hear everything from east to west! That is when he opened his lecture for Ismaʿil al-Bukhāri. He was a *walī*, but in sainthood there are various levels of ability and knowledge, so when that *walī* says, "When I speak, people east and west can hear," if a video camera can broadcast anywhere, can't a *walī* do that?

Throughout my childhood, by invitations of my father and uncle to world-famous *ʿulama* who came to our home, I never heard any of them speak even one word as great as Grandshaykh and Mawlana Shaykh ق! It is like comparing Earth and Heaven: there is no comparison! Just as Earth will end and Heavens are everlasting, saints' knowledge never ends.

When Grandshaykh ق offered food, we ate in the hallway next to the kitchen. We were ten people around him. Even if only a child was present, he gave a lecture for three hours. He often said, "I am not opening this for him, but he is a cause to open the *suḥbat*. I am talking to all *awlīyāullāh* and all *jinn* and angels hear it as they are in need for that *suḥbat*." I cannot repeat his *suḥbat*; they are very heavy. Sometimes we give from that as they open it, especially in Arabic when we travel to Indonesia. English does not convey the right meaning. Never has one of Grandshaykh's *suḥbat* been similar to the previous one, whereas our *suḥbat* are all similar in nature.

The Keys of Your Code to All Knowledge

In Madinat al-Munawwarah, when he was in seclusion, although he was always in seclusion, once Grandshaykh let Mawlana Shaykh Nazim stay in the same room. Mawlana Shaykh said from Maghrib time to Fajr, Grandshaykh never slept. Also, his food in 24 hours consisted of one small bowl of lentils, which he gave to Mawlana Shaykh while Grandshaykh only drank tea. He said Grandshaykh was in *munajāt*, standing making *duʿā* without pause for four-to-six hours, or even ten-to-twelve hours, and not one *duʿā* was similar to the other; whatever he supplicated was never repeated. I didn't speak yet about Mawlana Shaykh Nazim ق, I am speaking about Grandshaykh ق.

They received all this because they are the key of the code for all knowledges that Allāh ﷻ will open for His Servant! That key is one word. It is the key for everything, the key to Ṣirāt al-Mustaqīm. That is what the Prophet ﷺ urged his *Ṣaḥābah* to do, and *awlīyāullāh* encourage their students to do, and the whole Islam is built on it. It is *tawadaʿ*, "humbleness," as Prophet ﷺ said, "Whoever humbles himself for Allāh's sake, Allāh will raise him."

The Prophet ﷺ humbled himself and Allāh raised him in 'Isrā and Miʿrāj, so Islam is built on humbleness. Don't think about racism, as in Islam there is no racism; whether you are white, yellow, black, green or red, when you become Muslim you must forget everything you were built on, only show humbleness. Don't say, "He is white and they put us in slavery;" that finished when you became a Muslim, as the Prophet ﷺ said:

> *Mankind is from Adam, and there is no supremacy of an Arab over a non-Arab and no supremacy of a black man over a red man except in piety.*

Sincerity is only for Allāh. Don't say, "I am sincere and he is not." It might be someone is covering himself and he may appear insincere, but he is the most sincere to Allāh ﷻ. They want you to be under a test (so do not judge others).

Awlīyāullāh of such caliber live very simple lives and Allāh ﷻ raised them because of it. Whoever shows humbleness to Allāh, Allāh raises them. With what does Allāh reward them? He raised them in a Miʿrāj. Allāh gave the highest and best level of Miʿrāj to the Prophet ﷺ, from which some *awlīyāullāh* inherit a bit from secrets the Prophet ﷺ received in Miʿrāj. Do you want to be in Miʿrāj (Holy Ascension)? This association is a Miʿrāj!

Inna alladhīna qālū rabbunā-Llāh thumma istaqāmū, tatanazalū ʿalayhimu ʾl-malāʾikati ʿallā takhāfū wa lā tahzanū waʾbshirū biʾl-jannatillatī kuntum tūʿadūn.

In the case of those who say, "Our Lord is Allāh," and (who) further stand straight and steadfast, the angels descend on them (from time to time, saying), "Fear not, nor grieve, but receive the glad tidings of the Garden (of Bliss), which you were promised!" (Sūrat al-Fussilat, 41:30)

Those who say, "Allāh is our Lord Creator," will have equal! Do you say, "*rabbunAllāh*?" We are coming here to say, "*Yā Rabbī*! You are our Lord!" So that word alone, *rabbunAllāh*, is recited to humble yourself so that Allāh raises you. So we say, "O our Lord! We are your servants and slaves!" When they say "*rabbunAllāh,*" they put their first step on Ṣirāt al-Mustaqīm, then they stand forth. What did Allāh give them? He didn't say, "I give them one *ḥasanāt*," like when you do something good, Allāh gives you ten *ḥasanāt*: that is the entire reward and Allāh knows what reward He gives.

But when you say, "You are my Lord and I am your slave!" and put your feet in the direction of Ṣirāt al-Mustaqīm, what did Allāh say He will do? He said, *al-malāʾikat*, "countless angels," which could be millions, a hundred-million, trillions, only Allāh ﷻ knows. When those unlimited numbers of angels descend on you, they bring heavenly rewards and say to you, "Fear not, nor grieve, but receive the glad tidings of the Garden (of Bliss) that you were promised!"

That is for saying "*rabbunAllāh*" once. If you say it a hundred times or however many times you like, there is no limit on how many times angels will descend on you! So when *awlīyāullāh* say "*rabbunAllāh,*" it is not like when we say it; for them the Heavens open and they dress their followers with that.

This *suḥbat* is under the *tajallī* of that verse and is enough for everyone's difficulties and problems to disappear, so you don't need to say what is your problem. With that *barakah* of Mawlana Shaykh Nazim and Grandshaykh ق it is as if you are newly born, so all your questions will be answered through your heart, and Prophet ﷺ is watching everyone in his *ummah*. Every moment he is seeing and hearing, and he is asking Allāh's forgiveness on our behalf, as in the verse:

Wa law annahum idh ẓālamū anfusahum jā'ūka w'astāghfarullāh w'astāghfara lahumu 'r-rasūla la-wajadAllāh tawāban raḥīmah.

We sent not an apostle but to be obeyed in accordance with the will of Allāh. If they had only, when they were unjust to themselves, come to you and asked Allāh's forgiveness, and the Messenger had asked forgiveness for them, they would have found Allāh indeed Oft-Returning, Most Merciful. (al-Nisa, 4:64)

So we are presented to Prophet ﷺ through our *shuyūkh* and Prophet intercedes for everyone to take all their difficulties and problems, *inshā-Allāh.*

May Allāh ﷻ forgive us and may Allāh ﷻ bless us.

Wa min Allāhi 't-tawfiq, bi ḥurmati 'l-ḥabīb, bi ḥurmati 'l-Fātiḥah.

And with Allāh is success. For the sake of the Beloved, for his sake we recite the opening chapter of Holy Qur'an.

Know Who Is Written as Your Shaykh

Aʿūdhu billāhi min ash-Shayṭāni 'r-rajīm. Bismillāhi' r-Raḥmāni 'r-Raḥīm. Nawaytu 'l-arbāʿīn, nawaytu 'l-ʿitikāf, nawaytu'l-khalwah, nawaytu 'l-ʿuzlah, nawaytu 'r-riyāḍa, nawaytu 's-sulūk, lillāhi Taʿalā fī hādhā 'l-masjid. Atīʿūllāha wa atīʿū 'r-Rasūla wa ūli 'l-amri minkum. (4:59)

We are asking for support from our *shuyūkh*, from Grandshaykh ق up to the Prophet ﷺ. Every *ʿāmal* you intend—prayer, work, eating, drinking—that doesn't begin with you saying *"Bismillāhi 'r-Raḥmāni 'r-Raḥīm"* is *abtar*, disconnected; it has no value, as Allāh mentioned in Holy Qur'an:

> *Inna aʿtaynaka 'l-kawthar fa salli lī rabbika wanhar inna shāniaka huwa 'l-abtar.*
>
> *To you We granted the Fount (of Abundance); therefore, to your Lord turn in prayer and sacrifice, as he who hates you will be cut off (from future hope).*
>
> (Sūrat al-Kawthar, 108: 1-3)

The Childish Ego

Some members of the community of Prophet ﷺ said, "O Muḥammad! No one will be your inheritor!" It means, "You don't have a male child (heir), so you are disconnected, your name will not continue." A king has descendants who inherit kingship, so they were putting the Prophet ﷺ to shame.

Then Allāh revealed Sūrat al-Kawthar, with the meaning, "We have given you the river of Kawthar; therefore, pray to your Lord, as the one who opposes you is the one disconnected! You are not disconnected, as I raised your name with My Name, and you carried that secret, *yā* Muḥammad! You are the one I dressed to be responsible for the whole universe in My Presence."

So the Prophet ﷺ said, "Every *ʿāmal* you do, if it does not begin with *"Bismillāhi 'r-Raḥmāni 'r-Raḥīm"* is disconnected." Therefore, people have problems because we are human beings that forget; Shayṭān makes us forget to do what Allāh ﷻ likes. That is why in some Islamic schools of thought they say *"Bismillāhi 'r-Raḥmāni 'r-Raḥīm"* is part of Sūrat al-Fātiḥah, while other schools say Fātiḥah is by itself. However, that doesn't mean you don't read *"Bismillāhi 'r-Raḥmāni 'r-Raḥīm"* before the Fātiḥah. We do many *ʿāmal* in our daily life that don't begin with *"Bismillāhi 'r-Raḥmāni 'r-Raḥīm,"* and therefore, we are sharing them with Shayṭān and this puts us in difficulties.

There is no shyness in Islam, *lā hayya fid-dīn*. Many people in the west take a shower before they sleep together. If you take a shower before, that is no problem, but you must take a shower after. You were not clean when you were immersed in *dunya* pleasure and you must come out from it, so you must take a shower. It is very important when you sleep with your wife to begin with, *"Aʿūdhu billāhi min ash-Shayṭāni 'r-rajīm. Bismillāhi 'r-Raḥmāni 'r-Raḥīm,"* and then a good child will come. If you don't say, *"Bismillāhi 'r-Raḥmāni 'r-Raḥīm,"* that child will be disconnected and may face a lot of problems in life, because the *barakah* of *Bismillāhi 'r-Raḥmāni 'r-Raḥīm* did not dress him. That is why you see a child doing bad things. When you have intimate relations with your spouse, you must say, *"Bismillāhi 'r-Raḥmāni 'r-Raḥīm."* When you breast feed your child you must say, *"Bismillāhi 'r-Raḥmāni 'r-Raḥīm,"* and when you raise your child you must say, *"Bismillāhi 'r-Raḥmāni 'r-Raḥīm,"* or he will be raised with the bad reflections of energy that are around you.

Grandshaykh ʿAbdAllāh al-Fa'iz ad-Daghestāni ق said it many times, and it is in Sayyid Muḥammad al-Busayri's teachings on "The Blameworthy Childish Behavior:" *at-tifl an-nafs al-madhmūmah, man shabba ʿalā shay shāba ʿalay,* "Who is raised on something, even when he is old and his hair is white, he will be as he was raised." So it is very difficult when you are going to correct yourself in *tasawwuf,* or let us leave that word and say like Mawlana Shaykh said, in *"Rabbāniyūn,"* when you take the first step of *istiqāmah* on the level of *Rabbāniyūn*, you will not get rid of the blameworthy childish characters quickly, you must go slowly and you will not be dressed with *wilayah,* sainthood.

I heard this many times from Grandshaykh ق and also from Mawlana Shaykh ق, but he is now saying it is worthless to give these high levels of knowledge or heavy lectures. When he was younger he was so enthusiastic to give this kind of knowledge; he filled us, but in the last thirty or forty years he isn't speaking about anything but ego and democracy, subjects of the time, *hubb ar-riyasah,* love of being the boss. In democracy you bring the worst people into government, and they get the money and begin to govern you although there are millions better than them. That is what Mawlana Shaykh considers corruption, not as in the concept of *farabi* of democracy, as mentioned by one of the previous historians and a spiritual leader in *tasawwuf* who wanted to create *al-madinat al-fadilah*, "the most honored city." They teach that in each school of thought. We are not living in *al-madinat al-fadilah*, to pick the best one; now we live in ignorant civilization, not in "the modern world," as there is no such thing. What we are now in is the worst you can imagine of civilization and it is not going to improve, it will get worse and worse, until Allāh sends, as the Prophet ﷺ mentioned in many *ḥadīth*s:

> *Lā tanqaḍī 'd-dunya hatta yamliku 'l-arḍa rajulun min ahli baytī yamlā al-arḍa 'adlan kama muli'at jūra yamliku sabaʿ sinīn.*
>
> This Earth will not end until it is ruled by a man from the Family of my House who will fill the Earth with justice and happiness as it was filled with corruption. He will rule for seven years.

So until then there is no way to save this world. I was speaking with Mawlana yesterday after news of the Grand Mufti of Egypt giving a *fatwa* to celebrate the appearance of al-Mahdi ؑ! That is a big change, to mention in public that you can celebrate and wait for his coming, which means to prepare yourself, do not look at differences, whether Shiʿa or Sunni. So the coming of Mahdi ؑ is a fact, and to give importance to that is what is great. Scholars know Sayyīdinā ʿĪsā ؑ, Dajjal, and Mahdi ؑ will come. So what *awlīyāullāh* were preaching for a long time is now coinciding with what the Grand Mufti is saying. I am surprised. Once they published a book in Berkeley, California in which they referred to Mawlana Shaykh Nazim as "al-Mahdawiyya," which means we are the Sufi Order related to Mahdi ؑ, as Grandshaykh's and Mawlana Shaykh's preaching focused on that aspect.

Twenty years ago they were surprised about that and asked, "What are you saying about Mahdi?" Many Islamic newspapers have written about the Naqshbandis waiting for Mahdi, but now the Grand Mufti of Egypt—which means the Grand Mufti of the Muslim world as Azhar ash-Sharīf represents the Muslim world—the head of that is saying, "Yes, that is allowed." It means he is confessing that it is true that al-Mahdi is coming, what Naqshbandi *shuyūkh* have mentioned.

I haven't seen other *ṭarīqah*s mention al-Mahdi until 200 years ago in the time of Sayyīdinā Khalid al-Baghdadi ق, who sent his followers to Mecca to meet Mahdi ؑ. It means the Grand Mufti of Egypt wanted that to come out. Grandshaykh 'AbdAllāh al-Fa'iz ad-Daghestāni ق said it did not appear before that in the Preserved Tablets, but when Sayyīdinā Khalid ق came it appeared in the Preserved Tablets and he sent his students to Mecca to meet al-Mahdi ؑ and to give him *baya'*. They were dressed with the reality of Mahdi's appearance as they followed the order of their *shuyūkh*; it is a fact that they were dressed.

So you cannot get rid of the *nafs al-tifl al-madhmūmah*. The shaykh is in your life to polish you slowly, and don't think if you are polished you will automatically become a *walī*, because you are still in training. Like someone handicapped, you need many surgeries in order to stand. That is what I am coming to: Grandshaykh ق said, "A *walī* cannot be a *walī* if he doesn't clean his lineage all the way back to Sayyīdinā Adam ؑ, all his ancestors and grandparents. If he is able to clean all of them one by one, through that process he will be dressed with the first level of shaykhhood."

You cannot merely put on a turban, grow a beard and become a shaykh. No, you are an actor, not even an actor but an actress, which is not intended to humiliate the female gender but rather because all of us, in spiritual terminology, there is the "level of manhood" that even women can reach as there is equality in *ṭarīqah*, but if you do not reach that you are still considered to be in the level of womanhood. Real manhood is the level that someone is able to take away all the dresses to reach the level of Gnosticism.

For example, on a passport a woman carries the last name of her husband. Even in America and Europe, although they have the choice not to, most keep the name of the husband up to today, and the child carries the name of the father. That is your passport identity. They are following what is in the Holy Qur'an:

Call them to their fathers. (Sūrat al-Aḥzāb, 33:5)

The man plants his seed in the fertile soil that Allāh created. The honor of the mother is to give you a ripe fruit, but the seed came from the father. That is why you call them to their parents, as they carry your name. Therefore, how can a *walī* carry the name of his parent if his father is not clean? So to be a shaykh in *tasawwuf* is not so easy. The *walī* has to go one by one and clean them, and if he doesn't know his source he is disconnected. There are two lineages: one is physical and one is spiritual, and both of them are important. So if you don't know your spiritual lineage, who your shaykh is, you are *abtar*, cut off. If you are not connected to the right shaykh that is written for you on the Preserved Tablets, it is like waiting for water from a broken pipe.

The Genuine Shaykh Versus a Plastic Shaykh

For example, when you are a trustworthy person and faithful to your belief, you don't behave like Pharaoh, saying, "I am your Lord, Most High!" You are humble enough to say, "I am nothing," and to not call people to yourself and make them worship you, or prevent them from visiting the shaykh without your permission. There is no need for them to ask permission from you! I know of Mawlana Shaykh's representatives in America and other countries who give "permission" to their followers to visit him, which is not correct as anyone can go to visit Mawlana Shaykh!

Seventy years ago, Mawlana was young studied chemical engineering and then he left it as he didn't care for it. He had two *shuyūkh* teaching him Arabic and *tasawwuf* in Sulṭān Aḥmad Mosque. After a long time he said to Shaykh al-Lasooni, who had many students, "I want to take *baya*ʿ with you." He is a real shaykh, not a plastic shaykh; he is a real fruit. Plastic shaykhs are too many to count. We are all plastic shaykhs. May Allāh ﷻ take us from that 'plasticism' and donkeyness, and render us back to real fruit. Shaykh Nazim was very well educated and his parents were well-known in Turkey and Cyprus. When he said, "*Yā Sayyidī*, I want to take *baya*ʿ," the shaykh looked at him in front of thousands of students and said, "*Yā waladī*, I cannot give you *baya*ʿ."

Here you come and say, "Give us *baya*ʿ," it is very cheap. Bring as many as you can to take *baya*ʿ (for love of being the boss). Even if you have permission to give *baya*ʿ, don't give it, as the shaykh is looking at your heart and he knows its hidden aspects. If you give *baya*ʿ because you are proud, arrogant, happy or sick, the shaykh will know, "Are you calling them to yourself or to me?" Therefore, it is better not to give as that is from the bad character of the ego, which requires training to overcome.

Who is giving the *baya*ʿ? As soon as you commit a sin your *baya*ʿ is gone, until you ask forgiveness from the one you harmed; don't think it stays! That is why you cannot backbite or spread false rumors unless it is *haqq* and that person injured you, then you can expose them.

The shaykh said, "No, I will not give you *baya*ʿ."

Mawlana Shaykh said, "Please, *Sayyidī*."

He declined to give it and because everyone is not a *walī*, those who witnessed that began to think bad thoughts, so the shaykh let Mawlana go and his heart was broken. That was a test from the *walī*. It was not like today when people say, "Give me *baya*ʿ," even without *wudu*! We hope our *baya*ʿ is kept with Mawlana Shaykh. They keep it, but we don't keep it. When we sin it is broken and Allāh gave them that power to mend what is broken.

Some rumors are spread against me by different groups. I was in Cyprus and some of the Germans like me very much and are sincere, but there were two or three ladies in the ladies' section at the *dargah*, and one Friday they were reciting Sūrat al-Mulk, at-Tabaraka, waiting for Mawlana to give the lecture. I was sitting in the *mihrab* waiting to finish the prayer as Mawlana had put me as *imām*. We finished the prayer and went out. Then one lady came and told me two ladies said, "Shaykh Hisham doesn't give *baya*ʿ except for one-hundred dollars," to which she replied very harshly. Rumors and backbiting are prohibited by the Prophet ﷺ.

People heard the shaykh withhold *baya*ʿ from Mawlana, and it was test. Some people say, "The shaykh humiliated me," but that is how they raise your levels. If a plastic shaykh humiliates you, he is committing a sin by breaking your heart. If a real shaykh does that he is raising you, so don't have doubts about your shaykh. Mawlana returned the next day, as he didn't have doubts, and the shaykh said to him, "Nazim Effendi, your name is not written as one of my disciples. Your name is with Shaykh ʿAbdAllāh ad-Daghestāni in Damascus, Sulṭān al-Awlīyā. Go and take *baya*ʿ with him."

This is an example of *awlīyāullāh* knowing the hierarchy. They are not all with the same shaykh as there are various levels of shaykhhood, but whatever the level, still you must be humble and respectful. "Go to Damascus to Shaykh ʿAbdAllāh ad-Daghestāni. He is your shaykh. I cannot cross the border from Turkey to Syria."

It was World War II, and everywhere was bombarded as the French and the English fought in Syria. Mawlana Shaykh went to Homs and had to stay for one year, so he entered seclusion. He was studying the books of *fiqh* and that was the *maqām* of Sayyīdinā Khalid bin Walīd ؓ. He stayed in a room next to the *maqām* and listened to Shaykh Ayyoon as-Sood. Then the war ended and he went to Grandshaykh, but he didn't know where to go. So they dropped him in Hayy al-Meedan, it is very surprising they didn't drop him in Marja, the main taxi place, but they dropped him two hours from there! It was in the midst of war, no one was on the streets, and someone saw him wearing a *jubba* and carrying a stick like Sayyīdinā Musa عليه السلام.

Someone saw him and said, "What are you doing here, shaykh? Come, come, come." That one fed Mawlana and said, "How can I help you?"

Mawlana shaykh ق said, "I am looking for Shaykh ʿAbdAllāh al-Fa'iz ad-Daghestāni."

He said, "He is my neighbor! I will take you there."

The next day Mawlana Shaykh ق went to the door, but before he could knock Grandshaykh ق opened it and said, "We were expecting you."

Ṭarīqah is not easy; many obstacles might block you, but you must overcome them. Today is a shaykh said refused to give *bayaʿ*, people (do to their immense egos) will go astray, thinking, "That shaykh thinks he is better than me, so I will find another shaykh."

May Allāh ﷻ forgive us and may Allāh ﷻ bless us.

Wa min Allāhi ʾt-tawfiq, bi ḥurmati ʾl-ḥabīb, bi ḥurmati ʾl-Fātiḥah.

And with Allāh is success. For the sake of the Beloved, for his sake we recite the opening chapter of Holy Qur'an.

Imam al-Ghazali on Doubt and Submission

Aʿūdhu billāhi min ash-Shayṭāni 'r-rajīm. Bismillāhi' r-Raḥmāni 'r-Raḥīm. Nawaytu 'l-arbāʿīn, nawaytu 'l-ʿitikāf, nawaytu'l-khalwah, nawaytu 'l-ʿuzlah, nawaytu 'r-riyāḍa, nawaytu 's-sulūk, lillāhi Taʿalā fī hādhā 'l-masjid. Atīʿūllāha wa atīʿū 'r-Rasūla wa ūli 'l-amri minkum. (4:59)

We spoke about Grandshaykh's ق and Mawlana Shaykh Nazim's relationship, how they interact and how they lived very simply. I don't believe anyone of us can live such a simple life. That does not mean you will not try it, but this one (an African American *murīd*) and his wife cannot try it, because they believe white people used them as slaves. Let me ask a question: if Allāh didn't want it to happen, would it? If the whole world comes to make a person slave, they cannot without Allāh's will. There is wisdom in everything. Allāh wanted to plant Africa in America to show solidarity, so why object?

Lillāh fī khalqihi shuʿūn, "Allāh ﷻ has His way with His servants." Servants are like fish in an ocean, trembling, and when they tremble through Allāh's Order, it means they are not accepting, so they are thrown in the sardine can, where you see silver, black, white, and all kinds. Fish become smelly so they pack them in salt. Did they put salt on you or not? If they put salt on you, it takes all poison away.

If you go to someone's house and he entertains you very well, some will say, "*Masha-Allāh,* that is a *walī.*" That is how people think. Do you want *wilayah* from people telling you are a *walī* or do you want *wilayah* from Allāh ﷻ?

The Battle Between Doubt and Obedience

Sayyīdinā Imām al-Ghazāli ؓ, whose books are even sold in places where *tasawwuf* is not accepted, tells his story. "At the beginning of my matter, I was completely in doubt about everything—about Allāh, the Prophet ﷺ, Shariʿah, *tasawwuf,* until one day I took a shaykh."

The moment you accept a shaykh they put you on the right track, Ṣirāt al-Mustaqīm. Without a shaykh you are wasting your time. As previously said, *lā budda min murshidīn hissī,* the shaykh must be physically with you. "*Hissī*" means not only you can see him, but he sees you, he looks at you, you touch him; it also means *yatahasa,* (as in the *ḥadīth*) *inna lillāh malāʾikati yatahasasūn*, "Verily Allāh has angels that see (everyone)." Similarly, the shaykh is able to perceive his followers to bring them back to Ṣirāt al-Mustaqīm.

That is why you need a *walī* that is dressed with two dresses: a physical appearance and the physical ability to feel everything you feel. This is what we were taught in Grandshaykh's time; he taught so many deep topics. Now the teachings of Mawlana Shaykh Nazim, may Allāh grant him long life, are mostly mixed with cautions about democracy and the ego, but Grandshaykh ق taught us how to be in their presence. In his presence, can you look into the eyes of the shaykh? *Yastariqūna an-nadhar*, you could only peek, listen, take notes, then go home and study what he said. Did anyone here study? Today, as soon as it is written it is forgotten!

Imām al-Ghazāli ؏ said, the shaykh is the one that brings you back through his feelings: he feels you and can even see you. If he is in the east and you are in the west, still he can see you and hear your movements. Imām al-Ghazāli said, "Do you hear a worm moving on flat marble? *Awlīyāullāh* hear the friction between the worm's legs and the marble as if it is thunder!" So you can see theirs is not a simple power; that is why at any time they can reach anyone who is running away and bring him back. Many of these students who ran away in the time of Grandshaykh ق and Mawlana Shaykh Nazim ق returned as there is no choice.

Total Compliance Raises You

It is said that if you accept what the shaykh said without any doubt, even if it doesn't make sense to you, or if you disagree as it might interfere in your business, if you do what the shaykh said you might lose, but that loss will be a camouflage. If you accept it against your will, listen to the shaykh and follow what he orders, Allāh ﷻ will open wide a door from the other side that you did not expect, and He knows how big! But our *'itiqād*, belief, is weak and, therefore, we cannot listen or accept.

Imām al-Ghazāli ؏ doubted and did not accept, but he loved the shaykh. So slowly, slowly the shaykh was building up that love until one day Imām al-Ghazāli made the *du'a*, "*Yā Rabbī*! Show me something that is correct and I can leave these doubts." That night he saw Allāh ﷻ in a dream, Who said, "*Yā Abū Ḥamīd*, why are you running from Us? We are coming to you. Our doors are open, but you must come."

He said, "I awoke from my dream jumping with happiness!"

He woke up, prayed two *rakaʿats,* and ran to his shaykh, Yusūf an-Nassāj, to tell him the dream.

The shaykh said, "*Yā* Abū Ḥamīd, what you saw is the very beginning. Our blackboard is filled with our knowledge, but this is only from what is within you, we didn't yet give you knowledge from outside you, the *tajallī* knowledge. Tell me more of what you saw."

Imām al-Ghazāli said, "Allāh ﷻ said to me, "Leave this *dunya* through your choice before you will leave it by force (from a huge power you cannot resist)."

That is why in *ṭarīqah* the first step of the seeker is to know you were a sinner and to repent and make *istighfār*, asking Allāh ﷻ for forgiveness, and to regret what you have done all your life, to remember all your sins, which are too many. By making *istighfār* you realize your sins, then you need a huge spiritual machine to clean you. Where do you get that? "We have a door." *wa law annahum iẓ- ẓālamū anfusahum.*

You must go to Sayyīdinā Muħammad ﷺ; there is no other door! If you don't want to go, it is up to you; Wahhabis don't want to go and that is up to them. So if you have done something wrong or have difficulty, pray two *rakaʿats* and then sit facing *qiblah* and recite:

> *Wa law annahum idh ẓālamū anfusahum jā'ūka w'astāghfarullāh w'astāghfara lahumu 'r-rasūla la-wajad-Allāh tawāban raḥīmah.*
>
> *We sent not an apostle but to be obeyed, in accordance with the will of Allāh. If they had only, when they were unjust to themselves, come unto you and asked for Allāh's forgiveness, and the Messenger had asked forgiveness for them, they would have found Allāh indeed Oft-returning, Most Merciful.*
>
> (Sūrat an-Nisa, 4:64)

Then say, "*Yā Sayyidī*! You are the only door. Accept me through your generosity; if you do not it is your will, but please accept me anyway1" And there in Prophet's presence ﷺ, closing your eyes make *istighfār* seventy times, then he will make *istighfār* on your behalf, and then your sins are forgiven. Of course you will commit more sins and then repeat the process.

In the Naqshbandi Order you must get a shaykh that is not plastic, a real shaykh, or these doors will not open. At the end of *ṣalāt* when you say, "*As-salāmu ʿalaykum wa raḥmatullāh,*" you must feel the presence of your shaykh taking you to the presence of the Prophet ﷺ; if not, it means the connection is not working properly and you have to improve it.

You need a shaykh to guide you, but on one condition: that you submit in total compliance, *inqiyād lahu*, that whatever he says you answer, *samiʿna wa aʿtāna*, "We hear and we obey." Even if he says, "I saw in a dream that I have to slaughter you for Allāh," you must not only accept it, but with *inqiyād*, total submission. Another example of *inqiyād*: if you bridle a horse it follows where you lead it. Your duty is to follow, not to be like the horse that rears up in objection; you cannot say, "I don't want this!" *Inqiyād* means even if the shaykh takes you to a cliff, throws you over into the valley, don't object as still he might send hyenas to eat you! *Inqiyād* is to not have a will next to your shaykh's will: your shaykh's will has to work and your will must disappear.

Strong Belief and Love Lead to Submission

Imām al-Ghazāli ❁ continues his explanation, saying, you must believe that he is a *walī* and he is your guide taking you to Allāh's Presence. You must keep that *ʿitiqād*, belief, or nothing works. Grandshaykh ق said that *ʿitiqād* is what makes you follow the order of the shaykh and it saves you. That *ʿitiqād* will take you to Allāh's Presence, even if the shaykh is not of that caliber, still it will be opened to you because of your belief!

You must know he cares for you more than you care for yourself, and he will give you more if you obey. Here Grandshaykh ق is using this example. Let's say the shaykh ordered you, "Hisham, leave this project!" or, "Leave this *amr*!" If you believe what he says and leave that, he will give you something more precious, so don't underestimate the generosity of your shaykh. However, when you use your mind you get less or nothing. So whenever the shaykh says, "Leave this!" you must leave it, and when he says, "Take this," you must take it. He will not ask you to leave something except he will give something more precious. If the *murīd* does not believe that, it means his love is *nifāq*, hypocrisy: *fa in lam yaʿtaqahim kadhalik fa ʿitiqādihi nifāq*.

If the shaykh asks you to do something, you must do it perfectly or else you are doing it only for your benefit. If you have stayed with him over thirty years but you don't believe that he will give you something more precious by ordering you to leave something else, it means your love is hypocrisy and you will never benefit from his good character. That is why someone may come to the shaykh once, although *murīds* have been in his presence for thirty years, and yet he says to that new one, "You are shaykh of that whole city!" Why? Because there is more love in his heart than in those who were sitting all that time; theirs is hypocrisy.

Here are two examples. An Arab teacher who also writes poetry came to Mawlana Shaykh Nazim and stayed one week. We saw him on Sufilive reciting poetry for Mawlana and I was on the phone with Mawlana and we took turns reciting poetry and Mawlana was happy. The second time he went they told me Mawlana said to him, "I am putting you as *khalīfah* on Sham. What work are you doing?"

He said, "I teach children."

Mawlana said, "Stop that and go to all the closed *zawiyas,* Naqshbandi and others, and open them and make *dhikr*."

That was after two meetings and he gave him a long, long certificate of *'ijāzah* authorizing the work. Mawlana Shaykh saw in him something he didn't see in others. When you submit to *awlīyāullāh,* accepting what they say without coming out of the ocean trembling, you will get more benefit than anyone else. I was surprised when I heard Mawlana wrote that kind of certificate for him.

Another story is more important. Last year, Mawlana sent Shaykh Adnan, Shaykh Muḥammad, Hajji Mastan, a big guy from Turkey, and Aḥmad Yasin for *khalwah.* The best in seclusion were Shaykh Adnan and Shaykh Muḥammad; the others were talking and wanted to finish before the prescribed forty days, saying, "We cannot carry this!" Aḥmad Yasin is well-known for his background. Anyway, I was sitting at Mawlana's table in Damascus and Aḥmad Yasin came. Some said he shot a man in his leg and now Mawlana is so angry he called him to scold him! I sat waiting to see what will happen.

The food finished, the tables were cleared, then we prayed Ṣalāt al-'Isha. After that, Mawlana pulled out a long piece of paper and wrote a two-page certificate of *khilīfat!* Everyone was jumping out of their clothes, shocked that instead of shouting at him, Mawlana gave him *'ijāzah*! In such situations, what must one do? *at-taslīm wa'l-inqiyād,* "Surrender and comply." Mawlana was testing everyone through that person to see if they will surrender and follow his decision!

Imām al-Ghazāli ﵀ continues, "The shaykh cares more for the student than the student cares for himself." That is to show how much more we need to build our knowledge in order not to make our love *nifāq*, hypocrisy. Our love might be clean or it might be mingled with hypocrisy, which must be eliminated. That is the work of *awlīyāullāh,* to take hypocrisy from their *murīds*, while the *murīd* has to believe one-hundred percent whatever the shaykh said and promised him will happen; if not today, it will happen in the grave, so what is the big issue? Which is the more complicated life? In the grave you know where you are going, either to difficulty or to ease. But instead of that, go every day to the holy presence of the Prophet ﷺ and seek forgiveness!

Imām al-Ghazāli ؓ said, "If you don't have a shaykh that guides you, Shayṭān will guide you to places where the desires corrupt you." Where and how does your shaykh guide you? He has to guide every drop of your blood to where it must go! Also, Allāh ﷻ gave him the power to see and hear. That is from the *ḥadīth* of the Prophet ﷺ, narrated by Abū Hurayrah ؓ:

> *There may be a disheveled, dusty person who, if he swears an oath by Allāh, Allāh will fulfill it.* (Muslim)

Rubba ashʿath aghbar, There might be someone with curly greasy hair, with whom people are disgusted, but if he asks Allāh, Allāh will give him. It is not what is apparent on the outside; he is pious. So the duty of the shaykh is to fix the inside, and the duty of the student is to fix the outside. Keep smiling and be humble, that is good for the outside. If someone is humble and keeps smiling it is easier to be with people. I know someone here, if he wants to say one word he smiles, on the phone, in conversation, buying something, any moment he speaks he is laughing and smiling.

I asked him, "How is this?"

He said, "This is a university course they teach, so when you speak with people you are immediately acceptable." Did you hear that before? We never learned that.

Imām ash-Shāʿrani ؓ, the famous scholar of Egypt, said, "A lot of Muslims in Egypt believe in me and come to me to treat their various sicknesses. Do you know how I treat them? I pull one straw from the floor, give it to him and say, 'Go to the sick person and *bakhirū fīha*, make this like incense, burn it on coal and move the smoke around him. He will be cured.' They do this and they are cured. They think the straw cured them, but that straw is nothing. It is a psychological issue, so you draw their attention to something and their belief goes there. It is their belief that cures, not the straw. *Shifāʿ* is due to the *ʿitiqād* of the *murīd*, then Allāh cures him, but you must make him focus on something; without that he will not be cured. So I make them focus on straw or on a *tawīz* I write, and they believe in it and they are cured."

May Allāh ﷻ forgive us and may Allāh ﷻ bless us.

Wa min Allāhi 't-tawfiq, bi ḥurmati 'l-ḥabīb, bi ḥurmati 'l-Fātiḥah.

And with Allāh is success. For the sake of the Beloved, for his sake we recite the opening chapter of Holy Qur'an.

Attributes of the Real Murshid

A'ūdhu billāhi min ash-Shayṭāni 'r-rajīm. Bismillāhi' r-Raḥmāni 'r-Raḥīm. Nawaytu 'l-arbā'īn, nawaytu 'l-'itikāf, nawaytu'l-khalwah, nawaytu 'l-'uzlah, nawaytu 'r-riyāḍa, nawaytu 's-sulūk, lillāhi Ta'alā fī hādhā 'l-masjid. Atī'ūllāha wa atī'ū 'r-Rasūla wa ūli 'l-amri minkum. (4:59)

As we need this microphone for our voices to reach, also we need a perfect shaykh to carry us to the presence of the Prophet ﷺ. You may hear someone on TV but not without it; everyone must have a microphone for his sound to reach. *Awlīyāullāh* don't need this microphone, because Allāh ﷻ gave them a heavenly microphone to reach everyone from east to west. That is why to have a guide is necessary, because as Sayyīdinā Abū Yazīd al-Bistāmi ق said, *man lam yakun lahu ustadh ustadhahu ash-Shayṭān,* "Who doesn't have a teacher, his teacher is Shayṭān." Similarly, Imām al-Ghazāli ؓ said, "Who does not have a shaykh will fall into disasters," and, "Be careful of the arrogance of those claiming to be shaykhs."

There are many people who think they have powers, because the disturbance in their minds changes their way of thinking and causes them to hallucinate. Just as drugs might make you hallucinate, in spirituality, arrogance is a drug. When you are arrogant you begin to hallucinate like you are Pharaoh; you see lights, people moving around you, and you hear people talk to you, then you begin to order people and make them your followers. For this reason, be careful about those who pretend to be a shaykh. It is not easy to be a shaykh, as we have already explained.

This is translated from the book, *Talkhīs al-Ma'ārif*, "Summarizing the Knowledges," by as-Sayyid Hassan Hilmiyy al-Quhiyy ash-Shādhili an-Naqshbandi al-Qādiri, page 20-21. It has to be like a sign on our necks for everyone to read. A shaykh of the Naqshbandi Golden Chain said:

> Given the fact that I was born in a recent time (away from the time of Prophet and great scholars), and that I was in a weak state, and that I did not have much talent or great deeds, I was very lucky to meet great shaykhs and masters of the Golden Chain, to accompany them and to love them and be near to them. I was also granted to study with them, to wear their Sufi garment, to have their permission, to be a senior student of theirs and to have intimacy with them, as I will later

illustrate. I was granted nearness to them, and my wishes by Allāh's leave were fulfilled by them. Although I was not a good follower of theirs, and I did not emulate them in their deeds, and I deviated from their path, I still hope that Allāh will grant me their company in the Hereafter, and that He will grant me to drink with their cup.

They are the people whom if anyone sits with them, he will never have a bad end, even if that person who sits with them has dirty and filthy deeds. By Allāh's leave, I hope to have true love for them, and strong faith in their superior taste and sincere love. It was mentioned in the *ḥadīth*, "One ends up with whom he loves," and, "One ends up with the one he sits with," and, "One has the same religion as his friend." After all, a person's character steals from the shaykh's character, even if the ego rejects their manners.

Be the Blacksmith or the Perfumer

It means it the shaykh's character reflects on your character and people will begin to think they are looking at the shaykh. There are too many like that, whose manners dress the one who accompanies them. It is said, "Who accompanies the chosen ones, Allāh makes them like them." That is only by accompanying them. That is why Grandshaykh ق often said, "If your shaykh tells you to dig seven Earths down, that your trusts are there, follow the order, because even if you cannot reach, you will reach!"

Today, who follows the order? If the shaykh says something, you must accept. If you don't accept, then why do you spend your life with the shaykh?

Mawlana said something and I checked it, then I called and he was very happy, then he opened many things. You must accept because, "The *ṭarīqah* is whatever the shaykh sees." Before Grandshaykh ق passed away, he said, "My *khalīfah* is Shaykh Nazim, and Shaykh Hisham and Shaykh Adnan will help him." How many people rejected that? If you believe your shaykh is looking at the Preserved Tablets then you must accept, and you must go and speak with that one whom Allāh ﷻ appointed. Then Mawlana opened up a new explanation that was not known before; perhaps he was awaiting that phone call to see if you accept or not.

What are you losing? Nothing is changing, except yourself! If you follow the words of the shaykh, then you will be changed from worse to better. If you follow the Akhyār, Chosen Ones, then you will be of them.

Who sits in the association of the Chosen Ones, Allāh will make him from the class of good ones, but who sits with evil ones Allāh will make him from the class of evil ones, so choose which one you want to accompany. Grandshaykh ق gave this example: if you sit with a blacksmith, for sure you will get a spark that burns you and your clothes, and if you go to a perfumery, for sure you will get a drop that makes you smell nice, so choose!

How can we achieve being with them, to reach them, to love them and be near them, to wear their Sufi garments, to have their permission, to be senior students, and to have intimacy with them? What kind of journey do we need to take? It is simple. One of the *quṭbs* in that time, al-Aydarūs ﷺ, said, "Do you want to be in that journey and reach that? The only way to reach that door that takes you to spiritual realities is very simple, only one word, but that word is like a pregnant lady about to give birth@" It means if you want reality to come out, it has been in the womb and is now in the last stages of birth, like the perfect moon, to which there is no addition.

Al-Aydarūs ﷺ said, "Seeking that journey is through worship," as in the holy verse:

Wa mā khalaqta 'l-jinna wa 'l-ins illa li-ya'budūn.

I have only created jinn and men that they may serve Me.

(Sūrat al-Dhāriyāt, 51:56)

Allāh ﷻ didn't create us to eat and drink, but only to worship Him and nothing else. Even to sleep with your wife is worship. That is an example to tell you everything good you do is worship, visiting someone ill, giving water to someone thirsty, etc.

The *Ṣaḥābah* ﷺ said, "We saw something strange, one person going in the desert with no water and he was going to die. He found a well and went down and quenched his thirst, then went up, and as he came out he saw a thirsty dog that could not get water from the well, so the man filled his socks with water and helped the dog quench its' thirst." The Prophet ﷺ said, "Allāh saved that person from Hellfire for giving water to that dog."

This is the path and the journey, and how to face such things so that when one completes and perfects his *'ibādah* he will be granted different levels, *maqāmat*. As Grandshaykh and Mawlana Shaykh Nazim have said, between us and the Prophet ﷺ there are 70,000 veils of darkness, and that is why people are blind and cannot see him. You must remove those veils, which is not so easy. As explained in The Naqshbandi Sufi Way, *awlīyāullāh* begin to take from the back slowly as many veils as they can to raise your levels and you begin to acquire different levels in your journey. Now you are in level 1, then you move to level 2, and so on.

Power to Remove the Negative and Instill the Positive

You worship according to the power in that level and when you pass through all of them, *ahwāl,* trance-like states might appear on you, then you will speak strange things. A foolish person will not have such a trance, but be careful, as that might be a Shayṭān.

Then the state of your breathing will change, enabling you to exhale all negative energy from your body and breathe in positive energy. You will also be able to send positive energy to everyone around you by exhaling and inhaling. After that, it is a big transition to knowledge. So after you go through *ʿibādat; maqāmat, ahwāl* and breath, they open for you to receive *ʿilm,* knowledge.

So don't come and ask another time on how to achieve high levels of spirituality! If you follow them, you will reach and if you don't follow, you cannot. They are telling you what you must do. When you begin to get knowledge, they allow you to give examples and guidance, and protect the hearts of people around you. Then they begin allowing you to speak one-to-one to your tyrant soul, your ego, and that is according to the *ḥadīth* of the Prophet ﷺ:

Afdul al-jihād kalimatu ʿadlin ʿinda sulṭānin jāʾir.

The best jihad is a word of truth before a tyrannical king.

(Narrated by Abi Saʿīd al-Khudrī)

That "tyrant sulṭān" is a mixture of your ego, where ego is between your body and soul. You will begin to debate your ego, like looking in a mirror and speaking to yourself, and it is a *sunnah* to look at yourself in the mirror. The one who revives a *sunnah* will be granted the reward of seventy martyrs. It doesn't mean to look in the mirror to groom yourself to meet ladies, but rather to look and say, "Praise be to Allāh, Who perfected my appearance and my manners." You must look at yourself daily and thank Allāh ﷻ, saying, "Thank you for fixing my features and my behavior," and ask not to have evil behavior. If you look and thank every day, then you will be polished. Do you do that?

All this has to do with trying to keep good thoughts about others. Don't blame others for anything! Do *tafakkur*, contemplation, as Prophet ﷺ said, "To reflect on what you have done for one hour, you will be rewarded as if you have worshipped for seventy years."

So all of these are ready for you to take home in your heart and implement. Don't come to me and say, "I don't want to do work because I am superior," or, "They see me as inferior and themselves superior." Then you will have more and more darkness and negative energy. Good people say, "We like to help everyone and do the best for everyone." Some people ask, "Why do I have to do the worst work?" Because good people do the worst work! *Awlīyāullāh* do the worst job, polishing followers from their sins, so do the worst work! Today I will see if you are doing the worst or best work. Don't look at age, as age is a moment and that moment disappears one day, and everything that happened before will be gone.

Signs of a True Murshid

You must believe in the Muḥammadan characters, to accept and affirm belief of Islam and faith, and this can only be done by a shaykh who knows that journey, a shaykh who is attracted and loved, who says things people might not understand. That is why I had to call and check on what Mawlana Shaykh Nazim had said, to understand.

Awlīyāullāh are not here; they are busy somewhere else, and they must be *wāsilan mahbūbun,* who reached the love of and is connected to the Prophet ﷺ. It is very difficult to come to that stage. *ʿArifun bi 'n-naql wa bi 'l-ʿaqli,* "He knows the science of transmission and everything written (of Shariʿah)." From early stages to the time he reached, it means he knows every *ḥadīth* and every *āyah* of Holy Qur'an, and Allāh puts on his tongue what to say and at any time he can give you a *fatwa* from verses of Holy Qur'an and from *ḥadīth.* He is knowledgeable in Allāh ﷻ, in his self, and in all His Creation; he has to know everything about them and be present with them and absent at the same time, not showing himself there. That is a real shaykh, a *murshid!*

Where are those who call themselves "*murshid*?" Are they not ashamed to have their students call them *murshid* or shaykh? Run away from that title, because if you try to dress that on yourself without authorization, you will burn your followers and yourself. The real shaykh is the one who is both present and absent in seclusions; you see him with you but he is not with you, you see him in seclusion but he is not in seclusion. When he wants, he appears or does not appear in seclusion and when he wants, he does not.

May Allāh bless those *awlīyāullāh* and shaykhs. They say, "The sincere and pious one is with Allāh in every motion and in every stillness in his life." How can you show sincerity in stillness? We say water is still when there is no ripple or wave. So how that *walī* or Sufi who has been described, "The one who is always in the Presence of His Lord, in his every movement, with his praying and fasting," can be sincere in stillness? No one knows except that *walī*.

One day, I passed by Grandshaykh ق's living room window and saw him sitting, and usually he didn't sit there. He was still with his eyes and mouth open, sitting in the Divine Presence unable to move. I was afraid he would shout at me, "What are you doing here!" Light came from his mouth, his forehead, his eyes, his head, and the whole room was shining! That is the meaning of, "in stillness." For us it is still, but for them it is movement.

Taqabal-Allāh. The benefit of you coming here and spending two-to-three hours, no one can count except Allāh ﷻ. For us it is "still time" that has no beginning and no end, and it will be like that from now up to Judgment Day. At that time you will see who was sitting with you among *jinn* and angels. We are blind here; no one can claim he can see and if he does, that is only hallucination because only *awlīyāullāh* can see, only those who are granted by the Prophet ﷺ to be in the Golden Chain. This doesn't mean there are no *awlīyāullāh* other than those in the Golden Chain, but the Golden Chain is the highest level, the Sulṭān al-Awlīyā, who is the *ghawth,* and the five *quṭbs*: Quṭb, Quṭb al-Bilād, Quṭb al-Aqṭāb, Quṭb al-ʿAdham, Quṭb al-Mutaṣarrif, who are assigned that position in every century. Then there are forty saints in every time, standing at the threshold of the Prophet ﷺ, and 313 saints inheriting from different messengers, and then there are 7007 Naqshbandi Golden Chain saints.

May Allāh ﷻ forgive us and may Allāh ﷻ bless us.

Wa min Allāhi 't-tawfiq, bi ḥurmati 'l-ḥabīb, bi ḥurmati 'l-Fātiḥah.

And with Allāh is success. For the sake of the Beloved, for his sake we recite the opening chapter of Holy Qur'an.

Trustees of the Divine Secrets

Aʿūdhu billāhi min ash-Shayṭāni 'r-rajīm. Bismillāhi' r-Raḥmāni 'r-Raḥīm. Nawaytu 'l-arbāʿīn, nawaytu 'l-ʿitikāf, nawaytu'l-khalwah, nawaytu 'l-ʿuzlah, nawaytu 'r-riyāḍa, nawaytu 's-sulūk, lillāhi Taʿalā fī hādhā 'l-masjid. Atīʿūllāha wa atīʿū 'r-Rasūla wa ūli 'l-amri minkum. (4:59)

Verily on the Friends of Allāh, those whom Allāh brought near to His Divine Presence, *lā khawfan ʿalayhim wal-lahum yahzanūn*, there is no fear and they are not sad. (10:62) Someone who does not have fear must be special, because every human being has fear except Sayyīdinā Muḥammad ﷺ, as he is the Secret of Existence and he knows. Anyone else has fear in accordance with his level; we might fear a small worm or bug. Who is afraid of a cockroach must also be afraid of punishment, but we think a cockroach is more important than punishment, because *Allāh yamhil wa lā yuhmil,* Allāh delays until we forget something awaits us. May Allāh ﷻ protect us from punishment!

To be special is not something that comes easily. Some people are not afraid of cockroaches, spiders, snakes, and some are. How often did snakes come to *awlīyāullāh* in their seclusions and wrap themselves around that *walī,* looking at his head, waiting for any movement to attack him? But *awlīyāullāh* are never afraid, not from snakes and lions, nor from anyone except Allāh!

So He ﷻ is saying, "My Friends, the ones I dressed with My specialties, are never afraid," because they are His intimate friends whom He brought to His Divine Presence where there is nothing except Light that fills them with knowledge and unexpected manifestations of various secrets. That is why Allāh ﷻ said, "They are the safeguarders of His secrets." What kind of secrets? They safeguard secrets of importance and the Reality of Creation.

> *Wa idh qāla innī jaʿilun fil-ʿarḍi khalīfah, qālū atajʿalu fīha man yufsidu fīha wa yasfiku ad-dimā wa nahnu nusabbihu bi-ḥamdika wa nuqaddisu laka qālainnī aʿlamu mā lā taʿlamūn.*
>
> *Behold, when your Lord said to the angels, "I will create a vice-regent on Earth," they said, "Will You place one who will make mischief therein and shed blood, while we celebrate Your praises and glorify Your Holy (Name)?" He said, "I know what you know not!"* (Sūrat al-Baqarah, 2:30)

They complained, "O our Lord! Why are You going to create those who will make bloodshed?" He said, "I know what you don't know." He wanted to show the superiority of human beings, and thus He taught Sayyīdinā Adam ﷺ the Names from His secrets that He planted in the heart of His Prophet ﷺ, and that is why the Prophet was before Sayyīdinā Adam ﷺ in his Light, because first Allāh created the Light of Sayyīdinā Muḥammad ﷺ, and He put all the secrets in that Light, which He put in the forehead of Sayyīdinā Adam ﷺ, so he was carrying that Light. At same time, Allāh safeguarded all the realities of men and women, their essence/sperm, in the back of Sayyīdinā Adam ﷺ.

Who Are the Trustees?

Awlīyāullāh were in a state of worship in the back of Sayyīdinā Adam ﷺ, not only when they came to *dunya*, but Allāh also honored them to know the reality from that time. He said, *lā khawfan ʿalayhim wal-lahum yahzanūn,* as from when Allāh transferred that Light and secrets to the forehead of Sayyīdinā Adam ﷺ, *awlīyāullāh* received those secrets and were giving *bayaʿ* to their followers there, in the back of Sayyīdinā Adam ﷺ, who is an entire universe!

In the essence of their creation, *awlīyāullāh* were able to pull out that information. "He taught Adam the Names," refers to the secrets that were transferred from the Prophet ﷺ to Sayyīdinā Adam ﷺ, and from Sayyīdinā Adam ﷺ to *awlīyāullāh.* When that line was connected, from that time they were able to see they were in the holy presence of the Prophet ﷺ, which is why:

> *ʿAlā awlīyāullāhi lā khawfan ʿalayhim wa lā hum yahzanūn.*
>
> *Behold! Verily on the friends of Allāh there is no fear, nor shall they grieve.*
>
> (Yūnus: 10:62)

From that time they were made not to have fear, because they were given what others are not given: they were chosen. So when the angels complained, Allāh told them, "Don't complain in My Presence! Now I will give Adam more than you. I made him the safeguarder of My secrets." So Allāh is saying "I made *awlīyāullāh* trustees of My treasures." That means not even one smallest knowledge can be given without permission.

To be a *walī* is not so easy; anyone can be called a *walī* but few can actually be one. He must know what kind of secrets Allāh ﷻ gave him from that time, with what treasures he is entrusted from a little bit of what Allāh ﷻ gave to His Prophet ﷺ and what Prophet ﷺ gave to his followers. If one of these secrets were opened to this *dunya,* it will be covered with that Light!

Awlīyāullāh hide what is in their eyes. Sayyīdinā Shah Naqshband ق had so much Light coming from his face that to avoid expending power outside his eyes, the black pupils turned over the whites of his eyes. On Judgment Day, Shah Naqshband ق will be given permission to release that Light. When everyone is standing on Judgment Day, the Prophet ﷺ will say, "*Yā* Shah Naqshband! You have permission to fill Paradise as much as you want!" Grandshaykh ق said, "He will release that Light from his right eye and it will go and go and go as far Allāh likes, and then it will go straight and then perpendicular, and then back all the way back to his left eye. By himself, with that Light he will surround the number of people that will fill four paradises!"

Grandshaykh ق also said, "In the Diwan al-Awlīyāullāh, the Prophet ﷺ said, 'If Shah Naqshband ق can fill four paradises, can you not fill the rest?'"

If one *walī* asks, it is never rejected. Allāh ﷻ grants them what they request because He is happy with them and He wants them to be happy! May Allāh be happy with us.

Translated from the book "*Talkīs al-Ma'ārif,* Summarizing the Knowledges," pp. 20-21:

> They are the people of Allāh Most High, His special ones, and they guard over His secrets and the treasuries of His Lights. They are the inheritors of His messengers, the help and support of His Creation and His deputies in His Earth. Glad tidings to them, to those who love them and sought their blessings, to those who were mentioned in their supplication, who answered their call, who exerted themselves in their service, who safeguarded their sanctity, who took from their lights and their overflowing heavenly breeze, who looked at their faces, kissed the Earth under their feet, who was granted their intimacy, who witnessed the lightning of their lights, who was near their abodes, who accepted their advice and loved their stories, who caused mercy to descend by the mention of their names, who sought forgiveness through their love, who called upon them in their heart, who safeguarded them secretly and openly in their heart, who submitted to their ruling and surrendered all affairs to them.

They carry the burdens of whoever comes to them, because they are the carriers of burdens. If you have no burden or difficulty on you they are happy, because at least you made them easy with you and you didn't come with a heavy burden, you tried to safeguard them from it by making one less person come with heaviness, not to make them carry another burden. Always they are seeking whoever is in difficulty or under a big burden so they will carry that burden, but try not to make them upset and sad.

The Darkness of Complaining

I always saw Grandshaykh ق carrying so many burdens that he was not in a comfortable mood, then Mawlana Shaykh Nazim came and made jokes until Grandshaykh was laughing and happy. He said, "*Adab* is to make the shaykh happy." Don't bring stories to the shaykh that make him sad, as to complain in presence of the shaykh is unwise as it makes him feel bad. People explain all their difficulties. You don't need to tell your story because doing so means you assume the shaykh is ignorant of your needs! Therefore, only ask him to pray for you, because if he is really a shaykh he already knows your story. Just say, "*Yā Sayyidī*, pray for me," as he knows better and that is what they like, not to come and complain, "My son/daughter doesn't listen, and I am fighting with my wife."

Allāh ﷻ doesn't like complaining, nagging, and whining! The angels complained, then Allāh taught the Names to Sayyīdinā Adam ﷺ instead of the angels, so don't complain and you will get more. May Allāh keep us under their guidance and dress us with their beauty and their secrets that Allāh dressed them with so we may be with them in *dunya* and *Ākhirah*! Their secrets are opening more and more, because we are in times of great change, as *awlīyāullāh* and Mawlana Shaykh say, "Big changes are coming."

You don't need to ask for the proof as it is already there and you can see it. Yesterday, one that was on the throne of Earth, who previously spoke on behalf of all Muslims (i.e., deposed President Hosni Mubarak of Egypt) was in a cell lying on a mattress, and they judged him! They brought him from up to down!

He raises up whom He likes and puts down whom He likes.

(Sūrat Āli 'Imrān, 3:26)

After ruling a country for thirty years, now he is in a box. We must not shame or speak badly, or we will be like those whom Allāh ﷻ brings down!

This is a lesson, showing us where you were and what you are. May Allāh ﷻ not bring us down, not in *dunya* or in *Ākhirah*!

The Prophet ﷺ said, "O Allāh! Don't leave me to my self for the blink of an eye!" In the blink of an eye, that one came down. So we must take a lesson: not to fight with our in-laws and prevent them from seeing their grandchildren, as you will be responsible in front of Allāh ﷻ on Judgment Day. Also, some men prevent their wives from seeing their parents; you will be responsible on Judgment Day! However much you love yourself and your children, you must love everyone. Allāh ﷻ doesn't need you to provide for anyone as He provides for them, but Allāh wants you to share with everyone in their happiness and sadness; it means to feel with others. Why are *awlīyāullāh* different? Because Allāh gave them that ability to feel with others.

May Allāh ﷻ bring us back to awareness! We have no awareness, and leaders don't have any awareness that one day they will be brought down and their reputation will be bad and they will be humiliated. You are also a ruler of your universe and yourself. Don't let yourself be humiliated from being ruled by your ego! Prophet ﷺ said, "Say a just word in front of your tyrant ego." Try to teach yourself and polish yourself before they take you by force to be polished. May Allāh grant us heavenly polish to our hearts, because we are saying from here, "*Yā Sayyidī*! *Yā* Rasūlullāh! We are coming to your door, asking for Allāh's forgiveness and you ask on our behalf, as Allāh ﷻ said in Holy Qur'an to ask forgiveness for our sake!

May Allāh ﷻ forgive us and may Allāh ﷻ bless us.

Wa min Allāhi 't-tawfiq, bi ḥurmati 'l-ḥabīb, bi ḥurmati 'l-Fātiḥah.

And with Allāh is success. For the sake of the Beloved, for his sake we recite the opening chapter of Holy Qur'an.

The Heavenly Benefits of Following a True Murshid

Aʿūdhu billāhi min ash-Shayṭāni 'r-rajīm. Bismillāhi' r-Raḥmāni 'r-Raḥīm.
Nawaytu 'l-arbāʿīn, nawaytu 'l-ʿitikāf, nawaytu'l-khalwah, nawaytu 'l-ʿuzlah,
nawaytu 'r-riyāḍa, nawaytu 's-sulūk, lillāhi Taʿalā fi hādhā 'l-masjid.
Atīʿūllāha wa atīʿū 'r-Rasūla wa ūli 'l-amri minkum.

Obey Allāh, obey the Prophet, and obey those in authority among you. (4:59) We mentioned this *āyah* many times, and if someone says, "We don't need to write it again," that is bad *adab*. Write it every time, as you will be dressed from one of the secrets of that *āyah*. That is a heavenly dress, not like the dress we change every day and after one week we repeat the same dress. Allāh doesn't need to make a copy; each time He gives different manifestations and He creates angels for that verse that make *taṣbīh* on your behalf every time!

So each time we say, "*Atīʿūllāha wa atīʿū 'r-Rasūla wa ūli 'l-amri minkum,*" write it. If you don't know how, memorize it and write it. That is a *fā'idah*, benefit. We give a *suḥbah* by the shaykh's order, and so there are many benefits from it and, therefore, necessary for us all to take the main bullet points from it, to study and reflect on them. But our problem is that we are lazy. I see people writing and writing, they might have twenty notebooks, but ask them, "Do you read what you wrote?" No. That is the problem: we don't read what we wrote, we are only writing for *barakah*. *Alḥamdūlillāh*, that is a blessing, but to get a *fā'idah* we need to study the bullet points, and this is an important matter because when we benefit, then we can understand the relationship between what *awlīyāullāh* are saying and the *ḥadīth* of the Prophet ﷺ.

Awlīyāullāh understand every *ḥadīth* of the Prophet ﷺ and one of the most important a*ḥadīth* often mentioned is:

Yuhshar al-maruw maʿ man ahab.

People will be resurrected with the one they love.

This does not mean you will only be resurrected in *Ākhirah*, but also those who love each other will always be together and cannot be separated. That shows unity; not unity with Allāh ﷻ, as that is not accepted in Islam. No one can unite with Allāh ﷻ, and unfortunately many who are teaching *tasawwuf* outside of Shari'ah make these horrible mistakes, saying, "We unite with Allāh." Allāh didn't unite His Prophet with Him! He sent him to Qāba Qawsayni aw Adna, where he was very close but not united with Allāh ﷻ! Can human beings who use the toilet unite with Allāh? But for human beings to unite with each other, that is Maqām al-Fanā', the Level of Annihilation, which is the state of feeling what your brother feels and sharing in their happiness and sadness.

So the *suḥbah* builds love. When you are always in the company of your teacher, the reality of that secret will improve and produce the fruit we call *maḥabbat,* love. Those who are very near to the teacher give him *surūr,* delight and happiness. The shaykh will always be with them and they are always with the shaykh, even if far away. Even if they do not see it, the shaykh is always with them, as mentioned in the *ḥadīth:*

> *Lā yashqā jalīsahum.*
>
> *Never will someone in their company see a bad end.*

In addition, the shaykh has knowledge of every moment of their lives. It is said that one time people came to a shaykh and said, "O our teacher! One of your students died." In those days information was not sent through Internet; travel took at least one week by horse as it was a long way. The shaykh entered his room and went into *tafakkur,* meditation, about which the Prophet ﷺ said:

> *Tafakarru sa'atan khayrun min 'ibādati saba'īn sannah.*
>
> *To remember Allāh ﷻ for one hour (contemplate or meditate) is better than seventy years of worship.*

Meditation Will Raise Your Station

That means its speed is quicker than any Internet service today; you will be with the one on whom you meditate within seconds, much like the Internet today, only it is a heavenly Internet. So to meditate for one hour, and here "hour" means a short time, is better than voluntary worship. Imagine with one year of complete worship how much nearer you will be in the Divine Presence! That *tafakkur* will take you there in seconds. Do you see the huge power of meditation as mentioned in Holy Qur'an?

> *Inna fī khalqi 's-samāwāti wa 'l-arḍ, la-ayātin liūli 'l-albāb. Alladhīna yadhkurūnallāha qiyāman wa qu'ūdan wa 'alā junūbihim wa yatafakkarūna fī*

khalqi 's-samāwāti wa 'l-arḍ rabbana mā khalaqta hadha bātilan subḥānaka faqina 'adhāb an-nār.

Behold! In the creation of Heaven and Earth, and in the alternation of night and day, there are indeed signs for men of understanding, who celebrate the praises of Allāh, standing, sitting, and lying down on their sides, and who contemplate the (wonders of) Creation in the Heavens and the Earth, (with the thought), "Our Lord! Not for naught have You created (all) this! Glory to You! Give us salvation from the penalty of the Fire."

(Sūrat Āli 'Imrān, 3:190-191)

When you reflect on the creation of Heavens and Earth, saying, "O Allāh! You have not created this in vain," immediately all the secrets of the creation of Heavens and Earth will fill your heart and you will be able to see *haqq* (truth) and the difference between *haqq* and *bātil* (falsehood). Then you will be able to truly say, "O Allāh! You have not created this in vain." Just as in science, you perform lab tests to prove a theory; until then the theory is based solely on assumption and it might be right or wrong. Similarly, when you begin to reflect on the creation of Heaven and Earth, then Allāh will give you power to understand, "You did not create this in vain."

So when that shaykh received news that the *murīd* died, he reflected. Everyone was looking at the shaykh, asking, "Why is he reflecting?" Within a few moments the shaykh answered, "No, he didn't die." Although the news had come that he had died and everyone considered him dead, the shaykh said, "I have wandered in Heavens and Hell, and I searched completely in these moments and didn't find him there. That means he is still alive, so go and check." They searched and found him living! That is the meaning of *lā yashqā jalīsahum,* "The one who is with them will not see a day of sadness," as Allāh ﷻ gave them the ability to be with their followers: they are under observation 24 hours a day.

Don't think this is too much as it is not; in fact, it is something a first-class *walī* can do and not something *awlīyāullāh* run after. Anyone who keeps company with them will receive from their *barakah,* whether they are near or far, as long as you keep them in your heart and remember them, because they guide you to remembrance of the Prophet ﷺ, from which you will benefit and receive *barakah* from them and also many secrets in your heart. As soon as they get permission from the Prophet ﷺ, they will give you the code to see these secrets in one moment. There is a lot of classified material and if you are selected, hired, and given clearance, they will give you a code and then you will enter that and see all those classified materials, and in turn you will understand them and why they are classified!

There are *akābir*, the *awlīyāullāh,* the VIPs, and *asāghir*, normal people like us. So when a normal person accompanies a VIP, they go where ever the VIP goes. The VIP benefits as the normal one carries his bags and helps him, so the normal one is also benefitting. Both benefit mutually and this is Allāh's wisdom in His servants. That is why the house of a *walī* is never closed; it must always be open so that he benefits and those who come also benefit. If it is closed, why would he be a *walī*? Allāh gave him *wilayah* (sainthood) to give benefit to people. You will never see a *walī*'s doors closed; his doors are always open.

Five Benefits of the Relationship with a True Murshid

1. With just one moment of *tafakkur*, the shaykh can see all his *murīd*s and reach them; that is the first bullet point in *ṭarīqah*.
2. The second one is that normal ones, asāghir, benefit from the akābir, the VIP, and vice versa. Each benefits from the other, which is why the shaykh cannot close his door: the door of repentance is always there. If you do something wrong and ask for forgiveness, Allāh ﷻ will always forgive you.
3. You may have seen people performing their obligations, the five daily prayers, fasting, etc., but you may have also seen them doing much voluntary worship. That is because they are deeply in love with their *shuyūkh*. The love of the shaykh will make *murīd*s worship more, and that is what Allāh put in the secret of their love: the taste of love for the shaykh, which causes the *murīd* to worship more, which makes Allāh ﷻ and the Prophet ﷺ happy with them.
   That is why the author[2] said, *mā ta'abad al-muta-'abidūn illa bi maḥabbat mashaykhihim,* "The worshippers never worshipped more except due to love of their shaykh." Love for the saint is proof there is love for Allāh ﷻ, and so they guide you to the way to worship Him. Love for your teacher proves that you love Allāh ﷻ and His Prophet ﷺ! That is why we sit in Mawlana's association, and you must love all *awlīyāullāh*, not just Naqshbandis. There are 124,000 *awlīyā*. You love your shaykh more,

---

2 Of the book, "*Talkhīs al-Ma`ārif*, Summarizing the Knowledges,"by as-Sayyid Hassan Hilmiyy al-Quhiyy ash-Shadhili an-Naqshbandi al-Qadiri, which is occasionally quoted in this series.

that's okay, but love the others too. Don't attack other *shuyūkh,* love everyone and then you benefit from everyone. If you have good thoughts about them and you become familiar with their presence, for sure you will be able to reach the level of sainthood.

4. Imām al-Junayd ق (b. 830- d. 910, Persia), who came 200 years after the Prophet ﷺ, said, *at-tasdīq bi ʿilmina hadha wilāyyatun,* "To believe in what we say is proof of sainthood in you. We don't want more from you, only that; that is proof you are a *walī.*" Behold! Verily on the friends of Allāh there is no fear, nor shall they grieve. *Awlīyāullāh* never fear anything and they are never sad. al-Junayd ؓ said, they dress you with *wilayah* when you accept what the *walī* says and have no opinion, or then you will lose. If your shaykh said something, only say, *samiʿna wa ataʿna,* "We hear and obey!"
5. Keeping company with the People of *Khayr,* favors, as they are the People of Knowledge. If you sit in their association and mingle with them, it is accepted by Allāh ﷻ and His Prophet ﷺ, as Allāh wants people to know each other. That is why He ﷻ said, "We have created you all out of a male and a female." (49:13) "We made you students of that teacher in order to know each other and not to fight each other." That relationship is not to make you only accept your own opinion and no one else's. *Ṭarīqah* does not accept that selfishness from the Nafs al-Ammāra (commanding ego) that pushes you to do something bad. So when you accompany an *ʿālim,* he teaches you what to do, what is correct and what is wrong.

Reality and Its Image

Once they asked Prophet ﷺ, "Does a believer steal or rob?" He said, "That might be," because maybe he is hungry and doesn't have food, so he steals. Then they asked him, "Does a *mu'min* commit adultery?" He replied, "That might be." They might fall into the trap of Shayṭān. And they asked, "Does a *mu'min* lie?" To that he said, "No!" A believer cannot lie, because Allāh ﷻ sees you, so that means don't lie on what you promised Allāh on Day of Promises, that you will follow the Prophet ﷺ. There we said, "Yes, we will follow!" but we lied, as in *dunya* we are not keeping our promise.

What is the big deal if I say someone else knows more than me? If you humble yourself, Allāh will dress you. Many times, Grandshaykh and Mawlana Shaykh ق might have shouted at someone with very harsh words. What is our duty? Don't say, "How can shaykh say that?" Allāh ﷻ said,

"And of everything We have created pairs, that you may receive instruction." (Sūrat al-Dhāriyāt, 51:49)

It means, "From everything We have created two: the reality and its' image." The reality is always pure, but when the shaykh looks at the image that you made dirty, he has to use harsh words to take away that Nafs al-Haywāniyya, the Animal Self. For example, when a donkey doesn't move, you whip it, which is allowed. We understand whipping a donkey, but a horse is whipped to make it move faster or to tame it. You don't say that is domestic abuse; you whip the horse, but also care for it. *Awlīyāullāh* see the animality in you and whip you with harsh words so you will know what you are doing is much worse, but they praise Allāh ﷻ for your reality, as no one can touch the honor He gave to all human beings.

These quotations are important for us to understand *ṭarīqah,* as they are its main points. You must put them on a bulletin board or make a pamphlet with bullet points for people to see and understand. There are 124,000 *awlīyā;* if you collect one quote from every *walī* you will have 124,000 quotes! But we are lazy and want the shaykh to give us dessert already prepared, we don't want to even stir the pot. *"Y'Allāh,* make the rice pudding!" The shaykh gets tired of stirring the pot, so help him! Some students think, "Why does he want to be a *walī* if he doesn't want to work?" So when there is rice pudding, go and stir the pot a little bit and then you can take bites here and there before it is closed to you! Repentance is like that: as soon as you say *"astaghfirullāh"* you get some sweetness in your heart from it.

May Allāh ﷻ forgive us and may Allāh ﷻ bless us.

Wa min Allāhi 't-tawfiq, bi ḥurmati 'l-ḥabīb, bi ḥurmati 'l-Fātiḥah.

And with Allāh is success. For the sake of the Beloved, for his sake we recite the opening chapter of Holy Qur'an.

The Best Miracle Is to Be Consistent

Aʿūdhu billāhi min ash-Shayṭāni 'r-rajīm. Bismillāhi' r-Raḥmāni 'r-Raḥīm. Nawaytu 'l-arbāʿīn, nawaytu 'l-ʿitikāf, nawaytu'l-khalwah, nawaytu 'l-ʿuzlah, nawaytu 'r-riyāḍa, nawaytu 's-sulūk, lillāhi Taʿalā fī hādhā 'l-masjid. Atīʿūllāha wa atīʿū 'r-Rasūla wa ūli 'l-amri minkum. (4:59)

Here there is no teacher or student; all are the same. *Awlīyāullāh* don't differentiate between themselves and their students, and as we have learned from our *shuyūkh*, no one is better than the other.

People wear watches to know the time and to not sit being lazy, but time never listens to them; it is moving and we watch it move. We never saw time going backwards but we see it going forward, so time always keeps us up to date on where we are.

The words of *awlīyāullāh* are timeless and give us an awareness of where we are and how far we are moving forward. That is why looking and listening to the words of *awlīyāullāh* is as important as looking at a clock. Some people might listen once and then disappear for one or two weeks, then come back and listen a second time, then return after one month, leave and return. That is not going to work. Although people will be away from them and usually to be in the presence of the shaykh you must travel, Allāh ﷻ made it easy for you to read from notes of what they said.

Before Grandshaykh ق left *dunya,* he said, "When you want to address people, open the notes you have taken and read them, even one or two sentences, then *fuyūdāt,* a flow of information will come and your tongue will begin to speak. This means read what you have written, because, for example, if you are cooking food you don't put the pot on the stove and cook it for ten minutes, take it off the fire and then return to it after one week to continue cooking for another fifteen minutes! If you did that the food will never be cooked, but if you kept the fire even over a low flame, slowly, slowly the food will cook in perhaps one day.

For instance, if you want to cook meat until it is tender, put the meat in a pot with no water, add whatever you want of salt and pepper, then put it over the stove's lowest flame and leave it all night; in the morning you will find the meat is very tender and then you will say, "*Mashā'Allāh,* it cooked over a slow fire." If you cook it over a high fire, there may be a little bit of flavor but it will be chewy, so everyone prefers meat to be cooked slowly.

Similarly, *awlīyāullāh* prefer their followers to attend their *nasīha,* advice, and to take it easy. They said, *ajalla al-karamāt dawām at-tawfīq,* "The best of miracles is to be consistent in what you are doing." Miracles are only for *anbīyā,* but *karamah,* a blessed action that gives fruit quickly through the blessings of the shaykh, is like a miracle. To be consistent, we don't do *dhikr* 1,500 times a day then stop for two days and start again. Some people do 5,000 *dhikr* and then they stop. It is better not to stop but to stay with the lowest level, which is 1,500 times recitation of "*Allāh, Allāh.*"

Continuation of such associations are like miracles on us; they are not dead associations! If we have no continuity we are not benefiting. Today the continuity of such associations is available through the Internet, by reading your notes and by listening to the shaykh's recordings. That is what is important, then the food will be cooked slowly, and as it cooks you will see changes! Don't say, "I am not seeing anything." You are not cooked yet; you must be continuously cooked slowly, then you will see the changes. May Allāh bless Grandshaykh's soul and give Mawlana Shaykh long life, they said, "The best of miracles is the continuity in what you are successful," which means to continue what you are doing.

How to Fight Fatigue

Once Grandshaykh ق said, "If someone takes *wudu,* prays two *raka'ats,* and when he feels tired or sleepy, takes a new *wudu* and prays another two *raka'ats,* he will feel awake. Whenever he feels sleepy or tired, if continuously for forty days he takes new *wudu* and prays two *raka'ats* and then does whatever he needs to do, he will never need any sleep." If you really follow that procedure continuously, then at that time you will never need any kind of sleep, you will begin to feel awake, but you must not stop doing *wudu* and praying two *raka'ats* or else you will revert to your previous condition. That is why in many of his seclusions he didn't sleep, and his seclusions are not like ours of only forty days, but for one year or five years. He said, "I no longer need sleep or food."

There are some people who don't eat food and yet Allāh gives them life. It is not like someone who is on a hunger strike, protesting against the government by starving himself. *Awlīyāullāh* don't starve because Allāh ﷻ gives them heavenly food due to the continuity of what they are doing. They are busy with *awrād* and recitation of Holy Qur'an, and they keep their time full of Allāh's love and the Prophet's love.

Mā khalaqta al-jinna wa 'l-ins illa li-yʿabudūn. mā urīdu minhum min rizqin wa mā urīdu an yutʿimūn.

And I created not the jinns and ins (humans) except they should worship Me (Alone). I seek not any provision from them, nor do I ask that they should feed Me. (Sūrat al-Dhāriyāt, 51:56, 57)

Illa li-yʿabudūn, He didn't say, *yʿabudūn,* "one day and stop the next day," but to worship continuously. It is an affirming verb in the future tense that means it keeps running. *Mā urīdu minhum min rizqin,* "And I do not ask them to provide *rizq* for themselves; I provide for them."

Seek the Heavenly Sustenance

What kind of provision will Allāh ﷻ give them? From our understanding, it means Allāh will send people to help them, but the spiritual interpretation is that Allāh will provide them *rizq* as He provided the Virgin Mary. He gave that as an example—not in a prophet but in a normal person and in a lady—because in that society, men were held at a higher level than women. Allāh ﷻ provided heavenly provision to someone that was not a *nabī* or a man.

Kullamā dakhala ʿalayha Zakariyya al-mihrāba wajada ʿindaha rizqa. Qāla yā Maryamu anna laki hādha qālat huwa min ʿindillāhi inna Allāha yarzuqu man yashā'u bi-ghayri hisāb.

Whenever he (Zakariyya) entered her prayer niche, he found with her provision. He said, "O Mary! From where does this come to you?" She said, "From Allāh, for Allāh provides sustenance to whom He pleases without measure." (Sūrat Āli ʿImrān, 3:37)

What kind of *rizq*? Every time Zakariyya ق visited Maryam ﵍ there was a different fruit, not just simple bananas or apples, although the narration didn't say what kind of heavenly *rizq*, but it made Zakariyya come back and pray for a child. Grandshaykh and Mawlana Shaykh Nazim ق say that in the time of Sayyīdinā al-Mahdi ﵇ people will not need food, that one bite every forty days will be enough to keep them functioning with power! That one bite is to show you are in need, to make you humble, not to make you an angel. So as human beings we need food, but Allāh ﷻ will nourish you for forty days with one bite!

Do you receive the one bite on a plate? How do you receive it? It is brought to you by angels. You don't have to do anything, angels will appear and put it in your mouth, like when you put fuel in a car to keep it running, but here one bite keeps you running for forty days. Each bite has a special angel that allows you to run for the time between each bite. Each bite is different, depending on the time, moment and environment. Each person has a different bite that keeps you moving forward without tiring, because at that time Allāh orders the Earth and Heavens to give their power and you will be moving like a very strong wrestler who never gets tired. *SubḥānAllāh,* what nutrition that one bite gives!

In Indonesia, in the mountains you see old men and women still very strong, working in the rice fields, and they eat only a bite of rice wrapped in a banana leaf. So how do nutritionists claim that to maintain health we need a normal daily diet of 2000 calories and must take vitamins and supplements? Today everyone buys big bottles of them and they take ten tablets from this, five capsules from that, and manufacturers make more money. It has become like a pharmacy of alternative medicine. Those poor rice farmers eat one bite of rice in the morning and they are muscular, tanned, and working hard. What is in the one bite of rice? *Barakah*!

With *barakah* you get everything and when you truly understand the meaning of *barakah,* Allāh will open everything for you, when you approach Him through the Prophet ﷺ and you know Allāh is the One to bless you. You approach the Prophet ﷺ through your teacher and then every day they open new secrets to you. *Awlīyāullāh* understand that and then new secrets open to their hearts.

Do *awlīyāullāh* prepare notes before they talk? I never saw Grandshaykh ق write anything except once: he read Holy Qur'an and so on, but never wrote. Before my time he asked Mawlana Shaykh Nazim to write, and in my time he used me to write correspondence and the like. The one time he wrote it was the *tawīz,* the *ruqya* we all wear. He was ordered to hold a pen and by order of the Prophet ﷺ his hand wrote the *tawīz*. You can see his handwriting.

So *awlīyāullāh* don't prepare, the information just comes. The one who is clever believes in what they are saying. The one who wants secrets to open to his or her heart believes what they are saying as Imam al-Junayd ؓ said, *at-tasdīqu bi ʿilmina hadha wilaya,* "To believe in what we say is a level of sainthood." Do not to object or question; take it as it is. As Grandshaykh ق said, one bite is enough for forty days; don't question as your mind overanalyzes and may object. We have the example of these people in the mountains who are eating one bite of rice in a banana leaf.

Love of Awliya Reflects Love of Allah and His Prophet

So continuity is important, and to read Holy Qur'an is very *muhabbab,* likeable, but don't read it through once and then stop. It is better to read one *juz,* a thirtieth, every day or you can read one chapter or even one page. *Ajall al-karamāt dawām at-tawfiq,* "Don't do something you cannot do next day." Do what you can do each day. Read one page or one line; open the Holy Qur'an and just look at the Arabic characters on the page if you don't know how to read, and pass your fingers over the words as there is Light in those letters that is not found in any book! You may read millions of books in Arabic, but if it is not *ḥadīth* or Qur'an, it has no light of *Ākhirah.* Each word of the Holy Qur'an is shining with Light that will raise you more and more in your attachment to *Ākhirah.* Don't let Shayṭān cheat you! He is always after us and he is never tired and very clever. He whips his *shayāṭīn,* "Continue!" They are enemies of Mankind:

> *Wa laqad karamna Bani Adam.*
>
> *We have honored the Children of Adam.* (Sūrat al-Isrā', 17:70)

We break Shayṭān's head by reading Holy Qur'an! Even if you pass your fingers under the different verses, Allāh will be happy with you because you don't know how to read but are trying your best to learn. Those who know how must read and if you miss it one day then make it up the next day, so if you are reading one page, then read two pages, or if you are reading one *juz,* then read two *juz. Awlīyāullāh* also say if you cannot read Holy Qur'an then recite one-hundred Sūrat al-Ikhlās, or three, because *thalathat al-Ikhlas ta'dil al-qur'ān,* "Reading three times Sūrat al-Ikhlās is equivalent to reading the entire Holy Qur'an." So in your *awrād* if you recite one-hundred times *"Qul Huw Allāhu Aḥad,"* it is like reading the Holy Qur'an thirty-three times.

Look how generous Allāh ﷻ is with His servants! There is a great secret of the Unity of Allāh in Sūrat al-Ikhlās: "Say! This is My Holy Qur'an, My Words, Whose Essence cannot be known: that is Allāh, and The One with Ninety-Nine Beautiful Names and Attributes is Unique!"

Sūrat al-Ikhlās shows the Oneness of Allāh, so *awlīyāullāh* pull out their secrets from it. That is why they have many quotations from which to advise their followers. One such quotation is, *mā yataʿabad al-mutaʿabidūn bihā,* "Worshippers did not worship except seeking the love of *awlīyāullāh.*" How much they have worshipped is highly accepted by Allāh ﷻ, but more than that, what makes their worship higher is their love to their *shuyūkh* to *awlīyāullāh.* It means as much as you love your mentor, your shaykh, your master, your guide, and according to the love you show and the level of that shaykh, you will be raised like a rocket!

Li anna maḥabbata awlīyāihi dalīlan ʿalā maḥabbatih, "Because love of His saints is proof of love to Him," as mentioned in the Holy Qur'an:

ʿAlā inna awlīyāullāhi lā khawfun ʿalayhim wa lā hum yahzanūn.

Behold! Verily on the friends of Allāh there is no fear, nor shall they grieve.

(Yūnus, 10:62)

Love of the saints is proof of love to Allāh ﷻ and His Prophet ﷺ. As much as you love your shaykh, it takes you to love of Allāh ﷻ and love of the Prophet ﷺ. Your shaykh guides you to the way of the Prophet ﷺ, which is the way of Shariʿah and *maʿrifah,* but first comes Shariʿah. That's why, Allāh ﷻ said, "If you really love Allāh, *yā* Muḥammad, tell them, if they love Allāh, they have to follow your footsteps." And who guides you to the footsteps of Prophet ﷺ? They are your *shuyūkh.* So if you love them and His Prophet, then you love Allāh ﷻ. If you have good thoughts about them, if you find familiarity and are happy with their ways, then you will reach sainthood, as mentioned, "Anyone who accepts and believes them will become a saint and reach the level of sainthood." Don't have doubts or you will stay in one place!

Another bullet point/quotation: Keep the company of the people of religion, especially the people of *khayr,* favors and goodness, because to sit and mingle with pious and sincere servants of Allāh ﷻ is accepted and loved and in it there are a lot of benefits, *ʿajilan wa ajillāh,* some which will be granted immediately and some which will be given later, as you are progressing in their ways.

Since the condition to receive benefits is to mingle with them, be with them, listen to what they say for you will be loved, and then, as the Prophet ﷺ said:

Wa lā yazāla ʿabdī yataqarabu ilayya bi' n-nawāfil hatta uhibbah. Fa idha ahbābtahu kuntu samaʿuhulladhī yasmaʿu bihi wa basarahulladhī yubsiru bihi, wa yadahulladhī yabtishu bihā wa rijlahullatī yamshī bihā.

My servant does not cease to approach Me through voluntary worship until I will love him. When I love him, I will become the ears with which he hears, the eyes with which he sees the hand with which he acts, and the legs with which he walks (and other versions include, "and the tongue with which he speaks.")

(Ḥadīth Qudsī, Bukhāri)

Then Allāh will give you hearing different from everyone else: He will be your hearing and your sight, then *Allāh yajʿal waidhan min qalbik,* "When Allāh sees you asking and sitting with your teacher, Allāh will make a guide in your heart, advising you." Allāh will make a guide from within your heart, which means you will be guided in your way. Your food will be cooking slowly to become tender. So that is why it is essential to not be one day practicing and one day leaving practices; consistency is best. If you cannot attend the gathering, open your notebook and read. That is why we say keep a notebook to write in and then you can open it anytime and read and think on it.

They hire thousands of people to research and analyze in different languages what Shakespeare meant in his play, "Macbeth," when it is from his imagination. When you analyze the notes of *awlīyāullāh's* teachings, is it not better? But we are lost in the era of Facebook and YouTube. Yesterday when we gave the Jumuʿah *khutbah* against using Facebook and YouTube, one lady told me she was writing a paper on Imām al-Ghazāli and Googled him, but when she opened the page, on every side there was porn! May Allāh ﷻ protect us.

May Allāh ﷻ forgive us and may Allāh ﷻ bless us.

Wa min Allāhi ʿt-tawfiq, bi ḥurmati ʿl-ḥabīb, bi ḥurmati ʿl-Fātiḥah.

And with Allāh is success. For the sake of the Beloved, for his sake we recite the opening chapter of Holy Qur'an.

The Company of Saints Brings Righteousness

Aʿūdhu billāhi min ash-Shayṭāni 'r-rajīm. Bismillāhi' r-Raḥmāni 'r-Raḥīm. Nawaytu 'l-arbāʿīn, nawaytu 'l-ʿitikāf, nawaytu'l-khalwah, nawaytu 'l-ʿuzlah, nawaytu 'r-riyāḍa, nawaytu 's-sulūk, lillāhi Taʿalā fi hādhā 'l-masjid. Atīʿūllāha wa atīʿū 'r-Rasūla wa ūli 'l-amri minkum. (4:59)

Allāh said in the Holy Qur'an to obey Him, obey His Holy Prophet and obey those in authority, which means they are looking after your affair. As we said many times, there is no one higher than the other as all of us here are on one level; no one is the teacher as we are all students *inshā'Allāh.*

Allāh ﷻ also mentioned in Holy Qur'an:

Fawqa kulli dhil ʿilmin ʿalīm.

Above every knower is a (higher) knower. (Sūrat Yusūf, 12:76)

Above every *ʿālim* there is a higher *ʿālim* and above every knower there is a higher knower and above every teacher there is higher teacher. Don't think you are better because you are giving advice; think of yourself as in need of that advice more than anyone else!

Everything is hidden: you are hidden in the womb of your mother for many months, until Allāh's ﷻ will comes and you are born. After your birth many things are still hidden from you and slowly, slowly, you begin to try to understand everything, exploring your world so that you are able to learn. No one comes into this world ready-made; you cannot come from the womb of your mother with a PhD, you must study for it.

Granted Knowledge Versus Learned Knowledge

We are speaking on the level of *dunya,* but for Allāh ﷻ there are two ways: *wahban* and *kasban.* Through *wahban* Allāh grants to you, like a student grant or scholarship. When Allāh gives He doesn't ask you to pay. Those to whom Allāh grants are rare. Wherever they are and whatever they do they are dressed with knowledge. They come with knowledge and their eyes are open from the day of their birth, not the physical eyes only, but the eyes of their heart are open and they can see everything. They are rare like the most precious jewels, and to find them is difficult. All others must struggle to learn.

Why do we accept their knowledge? Here is a very simple example, but it opens our minds. When we want to know what is going on in the body we go to a radiologist. If a patient comes to a doctor and says, "I have pain here," the doctor may assume what is wrong and give him an injection, or he will send you to the radiologist to find out exactly what is wrong with you. The radiologist says, "Wait, we want to check the assumption the doctor has made." The radiologist doesn't want to make assumptions, he wants to see. You cannot seem but the radiologist can see. The other doctor cannot see; he needs the radiologist with his special instruments. With that special instrument we can see, even if we are not radiologists.

Similarly, there are two levels of *awlīyāullāh*: those who make assumptions about what you have and they might be correct or not, but they are still *awlīyā*; and there are *awlīyāullāh* with a special heavenly instrument to see what you have. That is why in previous times students did not sit in the presence of their shaykh without first taking a full shower (*ghusl*) and dressing in white clothes to present a spotless image.

As narrated in the *ḥadīth* of Sayyīdinā 'Umar ﷺ, in which he asked about the levels of Islam, Iman, and Ihsan, when Sayyīdinā Jibrīl ﷺ came to the Prophet ﷺ, he was dressed in clothes that are *shadīd al-bayād*, intensely white, with not one spot on his clothes, although he came walking out of the desert where normally a traveler is covered with dust. However, to come to the presence of the Prophet ﷺ you must be clean and this is an example for us. If you sinned, you must take a shower and sit facing the *qiblah*, coming to the presence of Prophet ﷺ and asking for forgiveness from Allāh ﷻ. Allāh will forgive you, but you must be clean.

Some *awlīyāullāh* assume and some of don't, because they have complete vision of what you need and, therefore, they treat their followers accordingly. The radiologist reports any defect so the other doctor can build his treatment plan accordingly, and without which that report they cannot treat you effectively. Similarly, there are lower-level *awlīyāullāh* that guess and assume the situation and they also give, but high-level *awlīyāullāh* give their treatment according to what they see. Both will be rewarded, as the Prophet ﷺ said:

> *Idhā hakam al-hākim fa-ajtahad thumma asāba fa-lahu ajrān wa idhā hakama fa-ajtahada thumma akhta'a fa-lahu ajar.*

If a judge gives a correct decision he will be rewarded twice, and if he made a mistake he will be rewarded once. (Bukhārī)

If the *'ālim's* or judge's assumption is correct, because he sees and he gives the right judgment, he will be rewarded twice. It is the same for the other *walī* who gives a prescription according to assumptions: the student will be rewarded by Allāh because he listened to his teacher and the teacher will be rewarded as he tried to give the right solution.

Another example is when the *Ṣaḥābah* asked the Prophet how to graft the palm tree and he told them how to do it. The next year it was dry. They said, "You told us to do this and now it is dry." He replied, "I did not come to fix your *dunya*, but to fix your *Ākhirah.*" It means, "Ask me something for your *Ākhirah.*"

So *awlīyāullāh* do not sit to fix your *dunya*; they might give you an answer which leads you to lose everything, or they might tell you to stop doing something and pray, or to help so many poor people, so don't ask them about your problems and come with heavy difficulties. Come and ask for their *du'a*, don't come and ask, "My wife said this, and I had this dream and another dream and another dream." What for? If you go to a president, you are lucky you have one minute to speak. So in front of *walī* don't speak too much, ask for his *du'a*, because they know what all your problems are and they give the advice that is most needed. That is why they say, "Our *ṭarīqah* is based on companionship."

Those Who Mirror the Pious

The *Ṣaḥābah* became companions of the Prophet by sitting with him, even if only for five minutes! As they sat in his presence they received what no generation after received, because they saw him with their physical eyes, and how much *awlīyāullāh* cry to see the Prophet with their spiritual eyes!

When the Prophet went in Isrā' and Mi'rāj, he reached Qāba Qawsayni aw Adnā, "the Station of Two Bow's Length or closer." Ahl as-Sunnah wa 'l-Jama'ah scholars agree that the Prophet saw Allāh with the eyes of his head; Imām Nawawī confirmed that. The Ṣaḥābah saw the Prophet and became his Companions, and the Prophet saw Allāh!

'Inda dhikr as-sulaha tanzil ar-raḥmah.
In the mention of the pious, pure ones, mercy descends.

Pious people sit in the Divine Presence and, therefore, mercy descends when you mention their names and when you sit with them you get mercy! We have said, "If you accept what *awlīyāullāh* say you will be with them; you will be a *walī*." However, the proof, as many ask for it, is what the Prophet ﷺ said:

Al-mu'min mirāta akhīhi.

The believer is the mirror of his brother (or sister).

When I look at you I see myself, because you became a mirror; you are so polished you reflect your character and good personality on me, and I see you in me. That is why it is said that deputies or representatives of *awlīyāullāh* begin to look like the shaykh, because of that mirrored reflection.

Grandshaykh ق told the story of a king who announced, "Who paints the best portrait will receive a prize from me." So the two best artists who everyone knew began the competition by painting on opposites sides of a wall. The day came for the king to see what they have done and award the prize. He came to the first and saw his painting was very nice. He went to the other one and saw him rubbing the wall continuously.

He said, "What are you doing? Where is the art?"

The artist said, "Wait, I will show you. Mine is better than his. To you it looks like rubbing, but it is polishing." You polish the rough surface of a diamond to reveal the precious gem inside worth a fortune.

The artist said, "Wait, you will see."

When they removed the curtain, the king saw one side of the wall was filled with very beautiful calligraphy and the other side was equally as beautiful: it was a copy of the other. Why? It became a mirror from his polishing!

Awlīyāullāh polish the hearts of their followers when you submit to them, just like the wall doesn't complain, "Why are you rubbing me so much?" That is why the shaykh may sometimes use harsh words as he is speaking to the animality in us to take it out. After polishing one side, it copies the other side.

That is why the Prophet ﷺ said, "The *mu'min* whose heart is polished will become a mirror for his brother." It means the teacher whose heart is polished will become a mirror for the student. As much as the student approaches him, that much his behavior and features reflect on the student.

So as much as you approach the *walī,* you will be resurrected with the one you love, as Prophet ﷺ said:

Yuhshar al-maruw maʿ man ahab.

Each person will be resurrected with the one he loves.

Also, if you are with pious people you will be like them. If you are with bad people, like through Facebook and YouTube, which many claim are the highest level of civilization, you are exposed to evil. If you are with bad people and take them as your teachers, their bad behavior will reflect on you. That is why you see many parents complain their child has become a gangster; those children become angry and proud with the character of a devil.

But if you associate with *awlīyāullāh, imān* will be reflected on you. To be in the company of *shuyūkh* and *mukhālata,* to mix with them and be in their association, has a tremendous effect on you in terms of receiving piety and benefit from them. They take you to the door of the Prophet ﷺ! But if you were not following the association yourself or you sat with corrupt people, you will become a follower of Iblīs and a bad influence on good people. Iblīs' goal is to take you out of *imān* and put you on *kufr*; he will do nothing worse!

That is why they gave us this quotation: *Li 'ṣ-ṣuḥbah wa 'l-mukhālata wa 'l-mujalasah atharun kabīr fi 's-salāhi wa 'n-nafaʿah, wa kadhālika fi 'l-fasādi wa 'd-darār, ʿinda musahābati wa mukhālatati wa mujālasati 'l-fāsiqīna wa 'l-ashrār.* "For the *suḥbah,* mingling and keeping the company (of sincere and pious ones) has a great impact on righteousness and for attaining useful benefit, but also on corruption and harm when associating, mingling, and keeping the company of the hypocrites and evil ones."

There are two sides: either sit with good ones and they reflect their good character and behavior on you, or you sit with corrupt ones and you become a follower of Iblīs. That is the biggest problem we are facing and we have to choose what we want. Everyone wants the good ones; others are 'gangs' and you know who they are. Those who are with the good ones, slowly, slowly their hearts are polished and their behavior improves, and they end up in the lap of the Prophet ﷺ!

That is why it is said, *wa lākin lā yadhhar marratan wāhid bal bi 't-tadarraj,* "It does not appear except gradually." When you mix with *awlīyāullāh,* don't think you get everything all at once; it is a gradual process that might take your whole life to achieve. Similarly, devils begin to tempt school-age youth, and by age fourteen and fifteen slowly spoil and corrupt them. They seldom return to the right path; the few who do are lucky, while the others are lost.

When Love of Goodness Takes Root, It Can't Be Cut

You must know that mixing and associating with people of goodness will plant in your heart *maḥabbat al-khayr,* the love of goodness, and this plant will never be cut. When they plant it in you by Allāh's ﷻ order that you are of the people of Sirāt al-Mustaqīm, the Straight Path, no one can cut it and it will grow, but you need to water it with *dhikrullāh* every day. So to water it, *awlīyāullāh* tell you to do your *wazifa,* daily recitations. The first *wazifa* is to read the Holy Qur'an and then to recite *salawāt* on the Prophet ﷺ, and then do your daily *dhikr*. When this is firmly established, no one can take it away.

However, if you mingle and mix with evil people, Iblīs will plant the plant of devils in your heart, which will make you love evil and being with evil people and doing what they do, as they reflect themselves on you. That is what we see now, they come to you through websites and little by little they spoil you with dirty things.

May Allāh ﷻ forgive us and may Allāh ﷻ bless us.

Wa min Allāhi 't-tawfīq, bi ḥurmati 'l-ḥabīb, bi ḥurmati 'l-Fātiḥah.

And with Allāh is success. For the sake of the Beloved, for his sake we recite the opening chapter of Holy Qur'an.

Journey to the Heavenly Presence through Rabitah

A'ūdhu billāhi min ash-Shayṭāni 'r-rajīm. Bismillāhi' r-Raḥmāni 'r-Raḥīm. Nawaytu 'l-arbā'īn, nawaytu 'l-'itikāf, nawaytu'l-khalwah, nawaytu 'l-'uzlah, nawaytu 'r-riyāḍa, nawaytu 's-sulūk, lillāhi Ta'alā fī hādhā 'l-masjid. Atī'ūllāha wa atī'ū 'r-Rasūla wa ūli 'l-amri minkum. (4:59)

Allāh ﷻ sent His messengers to teach us humbleness and discipline, and to tell us, "There is The One Who created you: all of you are His servants and He is your Creator." Also, He gave us all kinds of favors. Some people are able to see them and some cannot, it depends on whom they are with. If you are with good ones you will see and if you are with evil ones you will not.

Awlīyāullāh are trying to bring us back to see that by ourselves. For example, if you apply perfume often, your smell becomes nicer and nicer and slowly that fragrance disappears, then you put more, and as long as you apply perfume your smell is nice. However, the other group doesn't put perfume or any kind of incense that smells nice, because those who smell nice are in associations of someone who owns those fragrances and he is giving to them. That is *awlīyāullāh*: they are giving us every moment to dress us with these beautiful smells.

On the other side, the company of the other group will give you bad smells one after the other, until no one can approach you because you stink like a skunk and everyone must run away.

People don't like to sit with stinky, smelly ones, but everyone likes to sit with those who smell nice; they are *awlīyāullāh.* You experience their scent from far away because it is everywhere, attracting you to sit near them. It is said:

'Inda dhikr as-sulaha tanzil ar-raḥmah.

In the mention of the pious pure ones, mercy descends.

Fragrance of the Pious Is Everywhere

Just by the mention of good and sincere people, Allāh sends His *raḥmah* on you. That is a heavenly dress that smells very nice, and then *awlīyāullāh* come near you and angels approach you. However, but angels will never approach those who do not smell nice. As mentioned by Grandshaykh ق many times, the Prophet ﷺ was praying *tarawīh* with the *Ṣaḥābah* ؓ in Mecca. Angels descended with all kinds of rewards to dress the *Ṣaḥābah*, but that day Sayyīdinā Jibrīl ؑ was not able to come down, something was preventing him.

Prophet ﷺ asked, "What is delaying you, O Jibrīl?"

Jibrīl answered, "*Yā* Rasūlullāh, some of your *Ṣaḥābah* have broken their fast tonight with onions and garlic, and for that reason the angels are not able to descend."

Although garlic and onion is highly beneficial, and Allāh created them to cure you from seventy diseases, but despite that the angels could not descend. What then do you think of the smell of our bad behavior and character; how can angels come and take our *'āmal* to the Divine Presence? *Awlīyāullāh* are trying as much as possible to make your smell nice. Allāh ﷻ will dress you with a nice fragrance just by mentioning their names, and He will dress you more and more just for sitting with them, even if they aren't giving advice.

It is said, "Who does not benefit with his gaze, does not benefit with his speech." That means the first important meeting is of the eyes. The one who can benefit you by looking at you with his eyes for sure can benefit you by his speech. It is not necessary for *awlīyāullāh* to say anything. That is why Sayyīdinā Shah Naqshband ق had one silent session every week for three hours, in which his followers connected their hearts to each other, and in that way they were raised higher and higher.

Benefit from Keeping the Shaykh's Company

The presence of a *walī* in your life will give you a push up, to enable you to be in the Divine Presence and in the presence of the Prophet ﷺ. A *walī* said, "I saw the Prophet ﷺ in my dream and asked, '*Yā Sayyidī, yā* Rasūlullāh, what is the best *'āmal*?' He said, 'To be in the presence of a *walī*.'" That is one of the best *'āmal* you can do, because when you sit in his presence he will overtake you and will dress you with what Allāh, the Prophet ﷺ, and his grandshaykh dressed him and what he has gained from them, all without even hearing a *subhah,* only by sitting with him!

That is why it is important to visit your shaykh at least once a year. Even five minutes is enough to draw his attention to you and to receive his gaze and raise you to his level. The *murshid* takes away from your heart all kinds of weaknesses and puts all kinds of power in order that your connection will be stronger and stronger, and the more you sit with the shaykh, the more your *rābitah* is strengthened.

The Prophet ﷺ said, "Allāh has servants that if you look at one of them, that gaze will make you happy, after which you will never see an evil or bad ending." One gaze from them is enough to fill your entire life with happiness! It is said by Grandshaykh ق, that if there is someone even on a mountain top, a *walī* must pass by him once in 24 hours to gaze upon him in order to keep him strong and powerful. Don't think there are no *awlīyāullāh* among the *ummah*; they roam the streets like angels in order to support the People of Dhikr.

Allāh ﷻ has servants that if they look at someone they will give them happiness!

Also, to sit with a shaykh and look at him is far stronger than *dhikrullāh* because he will take you by the hand to his level. When you do *dhikr* such as, "lā ilāha illa-Llāh Muḥammadun Rasūlullāh," or, "Allāh, Allāh," you are doing it with your ego, but the shaykh will take you to where he is.

That is why *rābitah* is important when you are far from your teacher as when you connect your heart with him, he will take you to where he is. He may be in the presence of other *awlīyāullāh*, in the presence of the Prophet ﷺ, or in the Divine Presence! He takes you where you cannot go. This is why Sayyīdinā Shah Naqshband ق said, "Our way is through association and the goodness is in the gathering."

So don't pray alone and be by yourself. You may do that all your life, but it will not give you benefit. For this reason, it is best to be in the company of someone who can take you to presence of the Prophet ﷺ as he already has that Light in his forehead. People will surrender to the Light of *wilayat*, that Light that Allāh ﷻ gave to Sayyīdinā Adam ؏, to what He ordered angels to make *sajda*. They didn't make *sajda* only to Adam, it was in fact *sajda* of *ihtirām*, respect to the Light of the Prophet ﷺ in Sayyīdinā Adam ؏, as *sajda* of worship is only to Allāh ﷻ.

Therefore, for us to reach the Light of Prophet ﷺ we need to be with a *walī*. *Awlīyāullāh* inherit that Light from the Prophet ﷺ commensurate with their level, and it will raise you up to the power that *walī* carries; whether that Light is less, more, or unlimited, depends on his power. We will be lucky to find someone who is the highest among *awlīyāullāh*. Everyone says, "My shaykh is the highest," and since this is a general discussion we don't want to debate, but we say Mawlana Shaykh Nazim ق is Sulṭān al-Awlīyā! Anyone will be fortunate to find a sulṭān who does not sit on a normal chair, but rather he sits on a throne that Allāh gave from among the thrones He gave to the Prophet ﷺ. That means one of the thrones or levels Prophet ﷺ reached, he gives to that *walī* depending on their level.

So do *rābitah* and connect your heart with your teacher and *inshā-Allāh* you will reach the highest level of sainthood. Some *ʿulama* have said, *ʿalā qadar istiʿdād al-walī fa inna al-imdādāt ʿalā qadr al-istidād,* "The one connected with that *walī* will receive as much as that *walī* receives, stronger and stronger." And far as that *walī* ascends, he takes his followers with him. "O my son! Know the presence of a *walī* is important in your life because he will guide you not only by his speech and gaze, but by the power that Allāh put in the heart of his servant!"

The Kaʿbah within Your Heart

Awlīyāullāh make your heart your own Kaʿbah because, as described in the *ḥadīth* of Prophet ﷺ:

> *Ma wasiʿanī arḍī wa lā samā'ī wa lākin wasiʿanī qalbī ʿabdī al-mu'min.*
>
> *(Allāh said) My Earth did not contain Me, nor My Heavens, but the heart of My believing servant contained Me.* (Ḥadīth Qudsī)

They open your heart to connect you to the Light of Kaʿbah, so it becomes like a pipe flowing with secrets, knowledge, and treasures. You begin to see, hear, and envision all kinds of unexpected experiences when you connect your heart with your teacher. It will be highly beneficial if you find a very strong sulṭān that can take you to where he is. *Adab* must always be with the shaykh and you must not doubt what the shaykh says, even if you don't understand it. He is not going to cheat you as he gives us what Allāh ﷻ and Prophet ﷺ gave him.

Study these notes and try to fulfill them by reading from these notes daily. Check one after one and try to discipline yourself with them.

I will end with this very important quotation: "Connect your heart with a shaykh who is a manifestation of the *ḥadīth* of the Prophet ﷺ, 'The best servants of Allāh are those who, when they are seen, remind one of Allāh.' Keep your connection, *rābitah,* with those who, when they are looked at or seen, remind you of Allāh, and you say *'SubḥānAllāh'* and make *dhikrullāh* when you see them. *Inshā-Allāh* you will benefit from it. Don't keep company with devils whose behavior is not accepted by Allāh."

May Allāh ﷻ forgive us and may Allāh ﷻ bless us.

Wa min Allāhi 't-tawfīq, bi ḥurmati 'l-ḥabīb, bi ḥurmati 'l-Fātiḥah.

And with Allāh is success. For the sake of the Beloved, for his sake we recite the opening chapter of Holy Qur'an.

The Secret Treasure of "Obey Allah"

Aʿūdhu billāhi min ash-Shayṭāni 'r-rajīm. Bismillāhi' r-Raḥmāni 'r-Raḥīm. Nawaytu 'l-arbāʿīn, nawaytu 'l-ʿitikāf, nawaytu'l-khalwah, nawaytu 'l-ʿuzlah, nawaytu 'r-riyāḍa, nawaytu 's-sulūk, lillāhi Taʿalā fī hādhā 'l-masjid. Atīʿūllāha wa atīʿū 'r-Rasūla wa ūli 'l-amri minkum. (4:59)

Dastūr yā Sayyidī, madad! In every *suḥbat* we have to ask the one who has support, as without support the *nasīha* is not real advice; it will still be an advice, but with no light in it. When we ask for support, we show we are in need for them, and they come to us with power, sending to our hearts what to say.

Atīʿūllāha wa atīʿū 'r-Rasūla wa ūli 'l-amri minkum.
Obey Allāh, obey the Prophet, and obey those in authority among you. (4:59)

As soon as we say *atīʿūllāh*, "obey Allāh," from the power of that *āyah* Allāh ﷻ will immediately dress us as if we have obeyed Him on everything! In Holy Qur'an every letter has oceans of knowledge. As Grandshaykh ق and Mawlana Shaykh Nazim ق said, with every letter of the Holy Qur'an, even if it is repeated hundreds or thousands of times, Allāh opens 24,000 oceans of knowledge to His *awlīyāullāh,* which they keep hidden. They give to their followers little by little, like giving from a dropper. They give a little bit to the hearts of their listeners and continue to upload that until one day Allāh ﷻ will give permission to fully open it to the hearts of their *murīds,* perhaps when they are leaving *dunya.*

As soon as you say *atīʿūllāh,* "obey Allāh," it has a power and a secret. There are 500 *māmūrat,* obligations that Allāh ordered us to fulfill, and 800 *manhiyyāt,* forbiddens that we must leave. How to count and follow 500 orders and leave 800 forbidden actions? If you repeat that word alone, "*atīʿūllāh, atīʿūllāh, atīʿūllāh,*" reminding yourself with it, then Allāh ﷻ will completely dress you as if you have fulfilled all 500 obligations and left the 800 forbiddens. *Allāhu Akbar*!

Then you continue with, "*atīʿū 'r-Rasūl,* obey the Prophet," and with Allāh's order, Prophet ﷺ will dress you with all his *sunnah,* voluntary actions, and in the meaning of Khātam ar-Rasūl, "Seal of Prophets," as if you have obeyed him from beginning to end! When you recite *wa ūli 'l-amri minkum,* "and those who are on authority," Allāh will give you safety from the *ʿulama* of Islam and the normal authorities, so that you will never experience any problems with them, neither political or religious.

Safety and Fulfillment through Its Recitation

That is why Grandshaykh ق ordered us to write down that *āyah* (4:59), and he began each *suḥbat* with it: *Atīʿūllāha wa atīʿū 'r-Rasūla wa ūli 'l-amri minkum.* If we recite this 100 times a day, we will gain safety from Hellfire and safety in *dunya* from any problems. Allāh ﷻ will be happy with you and dress you as if you have done the 500 obligations and left all 800 forbiddens, and Prophet ﷺ will also dress you with his *sunnah!* Then someone with eyes that can see will see you are dressed with angelic power, as angels are always in worship, in prayer, in *sajda* or doing *taṣbīh*. So any *walī* who looks at you will see you as angelic, and you will not be less than that. In fact, in the eyes of a *walī* you will be higher than that, and this is only by reciting, "*Atīʿūllāha wa atīʿū 'r-Rasūla wa ūli 'l-amri minkum.*"

See Allāh's mercy on His servants! Unfortunately we forget and we don't follow it and this is our problem: we don't keep what Allāh wants from us. Don't think that an *āyah* from the Holy Qur'an does not have secrets. We read the *āyah* and think it has only literal meaning, but every letter of the *āyah* has 24,000 oceans of knowledge! If all of you here are *awlīyā* and let's say there are 100 people and everyone is a *walī*, as there are 124,000 *awlīyā*, Allāh will open to each one of you 24,000 oceans of knowledge for each letter, and it will be different from each person depending on the level of that person, as Allāh ﷻ said:

> *Lā yukallifullāh nafsan illa wusʿahā.*
>
> *On no soul does Allāh place a burden greater than it can bear.*
>
> (Sūrat al-Baqarah, 2:286)

Allāh will not put on you more than you can take. If your intake is stronger than someone else's, you will be dressed with higher knowledge and more power than him, but if he is higher, he will be dressed higher than you. So everyone will be dressed in a different way; it depends on how big is the container in the heart. If the container is big you will get more; if it is small you will get less, but in either case you receive by reciting, "*Atīʿūllāha wa atīʿū 'r-Rasūla wa ūli 'l-amri minkum.*"

Now when you recite the first time, you will be dressed once; when you recite the second time, you will be dressed twice, but this time it will be higher than the first, because you are repeating. Allāh ﷻ is not poor; He does not need to make a copy of the first. In the first time you will get whatever you will get of knowledge and spirituality, but in the second, third, or fourth time you recite, Allāh ﷻ will open to you different than before and every time you recite it will be different. *"Atīʿūllāha wa atīʿū 'r-Rasūla wa ūli 'l-amri minkum,"* is the head of all worship—*ʿibādat*, beliefs, *ʿitiqādāt*, and daily activities, *muʿamalāt*—as to obey Allāh ﷻ and His Prophet ﷺ is Islam. Everything that is included in *jamiʿah* is in that verse, so if you obey that will include everything.

When you recite it, Allāh ﷻ is dressing you from the Ocean of Obedience that never ends, because in every moment angels are in obedience to Allāh. Allāh will also dress you from the angels, and with whatever *tajallī* He dresses them through their obedience, the angels will dress you. Each angel is different than the other, so if Allāh ﷻ ordered angels to dress you by reciting, *"Atīʿūllāha wa atīʿū 'r-Rasūla wa ūli 'l-amri minkum,"* then you will be dressed in an infinite number of dresses.

So don't forget to recite daily, *"Bismillāhi 'r-Raḥmāni 'r-Raḥīm. Atīʿūllāha wa atīʿū 'r-Rasūla wa ūli 'l-amri minkum,"* as that will be your ticket to Heavens, not to the first or second Heaven, but to be with Prophet ﷺ, because you are obeying!

Allāh ﷻ dresses you with that obedience when you are saying, *"Yā Rabbī*! We are obeying You, we are obeying Your Prophet ﷺ, and those whom You have ordered us to obey." That will turn your whole day into a worshipping day, as if you worshipped the complete 24 hours, because Allāh ﷻ orders angels to fill up all deficiencies. So on the next day, when you recite another one-hundred times, *"Bismillāhi 'r-Raḥmāni 'r-Raḥīm. Atīʿūllāha wa atīʿū 'r-Rasūla wa ūli 'l-amri minkum,"* you will be dressed again, as if you worshipped 24 hours a day. Every day you will be dressed again and again. When you leave *dunya*, all of this will be uploaded to your heart and you will take them with you.

Street Markets Are Diversions of This World

Sayyīdinā ʿAbd al-Qādir al-Jilānī ق said, "This world is like a market of a few hours where you can buy anything you like, but at the end no one remains in it." He compared this *dunya* to a street market where you can buy anything you like, but at the end you will leave it. So we run all the day to gain something: if it is in obedience to Allāh ﷻ and His Prophet ﷺ, you will win *Ākhirah,* but if it is not in the way of Allāh and His Prophet, then there is a question mark.

May Allāh give Mawlana Shaykh Nazim ق long life, because he taught us how to save ourselves, when he said, "Who will pass by the street markets while his eyes are not attracted to its displays? Everyone looks inside the shops to see what they are selling, saying, 'If there is something nice I will buy it; if there is something good I will take it." Our eyes are attracted to that which will stay in *dunya.* So in order to make it easy for us, Allāh ﷻ said, "Recite, *'atiʿ ūllāh,'"* as reciting it alone has secrets, and saves us from the street markets.

That is why *awlīyāullāh's* knowledge is completely different from knowledge of academics or scholars. Scholars follow *qīla wa qāla,* "he said, she said." They rely on footnotes. If you write a book with no footnotes, it has no importance to them. They often speak of modernity or civilization and believe every ten years there is a new modernization of the community.

So the civilization which they say is evolving and provides you a much better life, as that increases, similarly, we can also say when you are looking for *Ākhirah,* it evolves level after level, going higher and higher, with which Allāh will be dressing you. So *awlīyāullāh* know there is progress in the hearts of people by reciting some verses of the Holy Qur'an, because not everyone will recite all the verses of Holy Qur'an. They know our weaknesses, so they give us one verse which has all the secrets!

Sunnah is to be dressed in loose-fitting clothes; any loose dress is considered *sunnah.* However, wearing loose dress does not mean you reached high spiritual levels, but to have discipline and *akhlāq,* good character, is important, as Prophet ﷺ said:

> *Rubba ashʿath aghbara law aqsama ʿalā allāhi la-abbarah.*
>
> *There may be a disheveled, dusty person who, if he swears an oath by Allāh, Allāh will fulfill it.* (Muslim)

Someone from a forest or desert may be smelly, dusty, and his hair is greasy, and you look at such a person and think he is homeless, but Prophet ﷺ said, "There could be someone like that, but if he asks Allāh ﷻ for anything, He will immediately respond to his prayer." His *duʿā* is accepted like lightning! If he asks anything from Allāh, He gives. So don't look at a homeless person or anyone with disgust, because he might be a *walī* coming to check you.

Islam is purity, discipline, and goodness. You may dress however you want, but is your character good? It is not only *dunya, dunya, dunya*; we need self-critique to improve. This *ṭarīqah* is not founded on money and business. There are some whose only thought is how to make a business out of being students of Mawlana Shaykh, how to fill their pockets; for them it is like a market. Try to avoid such greediness, and try to be like that dusty, curly-haired one who, if he asks anything from Allāh, Allāh will give him! That is what takes you to *Ākhirah* to be saved.

We are asking, "*Yā Rabbī*! We are weak servants, forgive us! *Yā Sayyidī*, *Yā* Rasūlullāh! We are weak among your *ummah*, help us! O *awlīyāullāh*! Help us and guide us to door of the Prophet ﷺ. The door to Prophet is *Ākhirah* and the door to *dunya* is money: choose, which one do you want? *Yā* Allāh! Show us the right door.

To give money in way of Allāh ﷻ is very acceptable. Allāh might even clean that money for you if it was earned in a doubtful way because you are helping. If you are looking after your family, your wife and parents, or help build a mosque, that is okay. Do as much as you can, because the intention to give is in your heart, but to cheat and build up your wealth on the name of Islam and, Allāh ﷻ and the Prophet (s0, and on the name of Mawlana Shaykh is dangerous! We ask forgiveness. We are weak servants and might fall sometimes, but we ask that they help us.

Surrender, Avoid Fitna and Make Your Shaykh Happy

Everything is built on good character and good manners. If someone has lost them, truly he is lost. Look at this one (*murīd*). *SubḥānAllāh*, he never changed since I knew him. He is very humble and has very good character. He doesn't raise his voice and he shows respect to all. With the *fitna* going around, with all what has been said here and there, he is safe, like the one whom I mentioned yesterday: a *Ṣaḥābī* ؓ who ate with Muawiya ؓ and prayed with Sayyīdinā 'Ali ؓ. The people asked, "What is this?" He said, "Sayyīdinā 'Ali's prayer will go to Paradise directly; therefore, I am praying in Paradise, and with Muawiya I am eating the best food."

So they try to make *fitna,* but they are not successful. The shaykh can test and appoint anyone, and our sole duty is to accept, not to deny. It might be a test, who knows? And there is not only one *walī* in the world, there are 124,000 *awlīyā*; there is not one powerful person and the rest are finished. So if the shaykh says, "I want this one in this place to be *khalīfah*, to carry responsibility in this area," we have to understand what it means.

When the shaykh says something, you must say "*alḥamdūlillāh*" and make him happy. You lose nothing. Mawlana is the sulṭān sitting and we are happy going around the world calling people to him, so what is the big issue? If he says, "This one represents me as my deputy," we say, "Yes!" What we are losing? But they want to make *fitna* and I am not yet exposing them; I am keeping quiet because what is the benefit? Stupid, ignorant people have no sense of spirituality and are after money only. Let them eat it in Hellfire! By their wrong actions, here they are preparing the wood that will feed the fire of Hell to burn them! Those who are creating *fitna*, separation and division, what do they benefit?

Allāh ﷻ said:

Wʿatasimū bi hablillāhi jamiayyʿan wa lā tafaraqū.

Hold fast to Allāh's rope and don't separate. (Sūrat Āli ʿImrān, 3:103)

Why are you making groups and trying to separate everyone? What is the benefit? If this one or that one is *khalīfah*, what will change? Nothing! And you are making groups and groups for what? If I open my mouth to say what I know everyone will run away, when they know the truth. But that is not necessary. I know things no one knows! I have been with Mawlana Shaykh for fifty years and if I open my mouth (on specific events) no one will stay, but what is the benefit? We have to keep Mawlana Shaykh Nazim happy. He used to keep Grandshaykh ق happy because he said many times, "Please don't tell me something that makes me sad," so we have to make him happy.

May Allāh ﷻ forgive us and may Allāh ﷻ bless us.

Wa min Allāhi ʿt-tawfiq, bi ḥurmati ʿl-ḥabīb, bi ḥurmati ʿl-Fātiḥah.

And with Allāh is success. For the sake of the Beloved, for his sake we recite the opening chapter of Holy Qur'an.

Awliyaullah Monitor Our Reactions

Aʿūdhu billāhi min ash-Shayṭāni 'r-rajīm. Bismillāhi' r-Raḥmāni 'r-Raḥīm. Nawaytu 'l-arbāʿīn, nawaytu 'l-ʿitikāf, nawaytu'l-khalwah, nawaytu 'l-ʿuzlah, nawaytu 'r-riyāḍa, nawaytu 's-sulūk, lillāhi Taʿalā fī hādhā 'l-masjid. Atīʿūllāha wa atīʿū 'r-Rasūla wa ūli 'l-amri minkum. (4:59)

D*astūr yā Sayyidī, madad*! This is a small space filled with big hearts. In the 1960's when we first went to Mecca, two million people came and there was no expansion of the *harām,* but still Mecca and Prophet's ﷺ mosque took everyone. As much as they expand, Allāh makes it lower because that place is for Allāh ﷻ and Prophet ﷺ, so even if ten million pilgrims come it will accommodate. Similarly, *mashā-Allāh* the space has expanded here. It was full five minutes ago but we were still able to accommodate more people.

In the 1960's and 70's, we used to pray Salāt at-Tahajjud and then Salāt al-Fajr with Grandshaykh ق in his room, and then went out to his mosque with Mawlana Shaykh Nazim ق, and Grandshaykh made *suḥbah* after Fajr. Here today we are following his footsteps. We hope Allāh blesses us with His endless mercy! Don't listen to me as I am not more than a normal person like you, and with Mawlana's *barakah* I am sitting and talking.

There was one *khalīfah* of Sayyīdinā ʿAbd al-Qādir al-Jilānī ق that used to give *suḥbah* after Fajr, ʿAsr, and Maghrib. Thousands of people attended his *majlis. Awlīyāullāh* are like spotlights or magnets; people are attracted to them even if they do not say a single word. How? It is Allāh's ﷻ wisdom; He put something in their hearts that attract people. Even if they are on the street, people want to stop and take pictures with them.

How the Sahabah Spread the Light of Islam

The cousin of Prophet ﷺ, Sayyīdinā Kuthum Ibn ʿAbbas ؓ, resembled Prophet ﷺ the most. He is buried in Samarkand, from where it probably took one year by camel or horse to reach Madinah as it is very far. Then there were no telephones, no text messaging or computers, no Internet, no oil, no money, or books for translation. He was just one person, but after Prophet ﷺ left *dunya,* with Prophet's ﷺ inspiration in his heart he headed to Samarkand. He was not originally from that area and yet he was between them. There were no relatives with him, but he turned Central Asia to Islam by himself. How? He was not familiar with the language; he spoke Arabic, but without speaking with the tongue, the heart spoke. He had a light in his face that attracts anyone, so slowly, slowly, without talking, with what today they call 'telepathy' he spoke heart-to-heart, looking into his heart, releasing that light carrying all kind of knowledge, putting change in their hearts in a minute.

Don't ask how. The light released from his heart is like an electro-magnetic wave. When we speak, we release that and the ears hear it. He sent that to the ears of their hearts and they were able to take it because the *barakah* of his presence. Don't ask how! This small telephone takes that sound immediately and turns it into a small storage space, so couldn't a Ṣaḥābī do that? He was under the teaching of Prophet ﷺ and brought everyone to Islam because of the Light of Prophet ﷺ that was in his forehead. Prophet ﷺ gave everyone something special. Don't deny it; we will be wrong to do that as Prophet ﷺ is with everyone.

W ʿalamū anna fīkum Rasūlullāh.

And know Allāh's Messenger is in you. (Sūrat al-Hujurāt, 49:7)

His power and his Light are in you; all you must do to access it is make *tafakkur*, meditation or contemplation. Zoom in yourself as much as you can to make it sharp. If you take a flashlight and narrow it further and further, it will become a very strong laser.

Another example is, if you put a magnifying glass in direct sunlight, the light zooms through the magnifying glass and burns paper, whereas if you put the paper under the sun by itself it will not burn. *Awlīyāullāh* have a heavenly magnifying glass in their hearts; they release that power through their foreheads. From there they direct it to the intended person, who will respond and immediately. *Awlīyāullāh* carry a strong and powerful light that can move mountains and that is not too much for them!

You cannot lift a block of iron that weighs a ton, but with a crane you can. How does the crane carry a ton or ten tons of iron? The crane is producing a high energy through its engine that enables it to move the iron up or down. The crane is *dunya* energy and *awlīyāullāh* have heavenly energy. Therefore, it is not strange for *awlīyāullāh* to move the hearts of people. So what then do you think of a Ṣaḥābī? Prophet ﷺ sent his *Ṣaḥābah* ﷺ everywhere and they spread Islam with only their presence. Their hearts were like a magnet or a magnifying glass; they can move it the way they like and zoom in and burn your love of *dunya.*

When your love of *dunya* is burned, *Ākhirah* appears by itself, because from the beginning of time there has always been a struggle between good and evil. Throughout history, the bad wanted to attack the good, but when *bātil* vanishes, *haqq* comes.

Wa qul ja'a al-haqq wa zahaqa al-bātil inna 'l-bātila kāna zahūqa.

Say (O Muḥammad), "Haqq (truth) has come and bātil (falsehood) has perished." (Sūrat al-Isrā, 17:81)

The Grant of Heavenly Knowledge and Your Amanat

So when *Ākhirah* comes you see your heart change. What attracts you to come here? Your love to *Ākhirah,* to *awlīyāullāh,* to Mawlana Shaykh Nazim ق and Prophet ﷺ. We are not doing any kind of business here; instead, we hope we are doing some business for *Ākhirah* so that Allāh ﷻ will shower us with His Mercy!

Wa law istiqāmū ʿalā aṭ-ṭarīqati la-asqaynāhum mā'an ghadaqa.

If they had (only) remained on the (right) Way, We would certainly have bestowed on them rain in abundance. (Sūrat al-Jinn, 72:16)

It means if they keep their ways on Ṣirāt al-Mustaqīm. This is the only place in the Holy Qur'an where *ṭarīqah* is mentioned by name. "If they keep their belief and faith on the way, *ṭarīqah,* We will *ma'an ghadaqa,* shower them with abundant rain," with water, meaning, "We will give them lots of water to drink." What is water?

Wa jaʿalna min al-mā'i kulla shay'in hayy.

We made from water every living thing. (Sūrat al-Anbīyā, 21:30)

This means if you stay on *ṭarīqah* you will rejuvenate your heart because you are moving on the Straight Path. The Prophet ﷺ mentioned:

Man ʿāmala bimā yaʿalam awrathahullāhū ʿilma lam yaʿalam.

Who does something according to what he learned, Allāh will give him knowledge that he did not learn.

When you teach from what you have learned, as we are sitting here teaching, Allāh will give you knowledge that you did not learn. It means you do your job according to what you have learned.

Lā yukallifullāh nafsan illa wus'ahā.

On no soul does Allāh place a burden greater than it can bear.

(Sūrat al-Baqarah, 2:286)

Allāh does not ask you to do more than your capacity; He doesn't burden you. Allāh is "ar-Raḥmān, ar-Raḥīm," and He gives according to what you can take. This means if you are sitting with a teacher or with someone at a higher level, a *walī,* Sulṭān al-Awlīyā or even higher, like *Ṣaḥābah* sat with Prophet ﷺ, Allāh will give you what you did not learn, but on the condition that you do not object. The example of this is, Sayyīdinā Musa ؑ was sent as a messenger and yet he wanted to learn more and he found one of the many servants of Allāh ﷻ.

Fawajada 'abdan min 'ibādīna ataynahū raḥmatan min 'indina wa 'allamnahū min ladunna 'ilma.

So they found one of Our servants on whom We had bestowed mercy from Ourselves and whom We had taught knowledge from Our own Presence.

(Sūrat al-Kahf, 18:65)

The term "'*abd*" is mentioned in many *seerahs,* and it is Sayyīdinā al-Khidr ؑ, about whom Allāh ﷻ said, "We gave him *raḥmah.*" He didn't say, "We gave him heavenly knowledge (first)," He said, "We gave him *raḥmah* (first)," to prepare him to receive knowledge. You cannot claim to receive knowledge before you are receiving mercy; first you will receive mercy and then knowledge.

Who is the mercy for Khidr ؑ? It is Prophet ﷺ. If Prophet ﷺ did not dress Sayyīdinā Khidr ؑ with what Allāh gave him, he would never have received knowledge.

Wa mā arsalnāka illa raḥmatan lil-'alāmīn.

(O Muḥammad!) We have not sent you except as a Mercy for all the Worlds.

(Sūrat al-Anbīyā, 21:107)

So Sayyīdinā al-Khidr ؑ was in the Prophet's presence in a spiritual light, learning from him. Then after he was given his *amānāt,* trust, he was able to receive heavenly knowledge that no one can understand. That's why you cannot reach heavenly knowledge without a guide, because that guide is dressed from Prophet ﷺ with that *raḥmah* to prepare you. You cannot do it by yourself, it has to be from a guide. If you are with a guide for many years and he wants to give you your *amānāt*, it cannot be activated without the presence of Prophet ﷺ; he must approve that you are clean or else it will not work. If Prophet ﷺ certifies to your shaykh that you are alright, the *amānāt* codes will be given and you will move in them.

The example is the story of Grandshaykh ق, who said, "Once, by the order of Prophet ﷺ, I ordered Shaykh Nazim to seclusion for nine months in Madinatu 'l-Munawwara, and to make the five prayers in Harām an-Nabawi ﷺ every day. Going there, he must only look down at his feet with no permission to look around. As Shaykh Nazim emerged from the Harām on the last day of his seclusion, me, Sayyīdinā Abū Bakr ؓ and Prophet ﷺ were watching him. I said, '*Yā Sayyidī*! Your son has completed seclusion. May we give him his *amānāt*?'"

If Prophet ﷺ, Sayyīdinā Abū Bakr ؓ, and Sayyīdinā Shah Naqshband ق are not present, the shaykh cannot give the *murīd* his *amānāt*. People think everything is simple, but it is not. As soon as a shaykh says, "You have permission on this," you became a big *walī*. They have to crush you like olives to make oil and then throw you to the dogs to eat you, then they can give you your *amānāt*!

Grandshaykh continued, "Prophet ﷺ replied, 'No, don't give the *amānāt* yet because he still sees himself.'" *SubḥānAllāh*, it was a test! Grandshaykh said to Mawlana Shaykh Nazim, "*Yā waladī*, I am disappointed." They may say something to see how you or others react. Others might think, "Oh, this is a bad person." They are wrong! It means the shaykh is polishing you to see how you react, but that is hidden. The shaykh says something but means something else, and this story is a good example.

Today, Mawlana Shaykh says something to people and they immediately put it on the Internet. They want to see your reaction: do you accept and believe, or not? He may humiliate you by saying something and then check you. So Grandshaykh ق said, "You disappointed me, as you depended on your *'āmal* too much."

That was the key for Mawlana Shaykh Nazim to get his *amānāt;* Grandshaykh told this privately to me and my brother. "Shaykh Nazim answered, '*Yā Sayyidī*! How am I not going to be proud of myself? Can someone who has a shaykh like you not be proud of himself?' As soon as he said that, Prophet ﷺ gave him his *amānāt*." They wanted him to admit that it's coming from his teacher, not from him.

If Mawlana Shaykh says, "Your shaykh is this stone," you must accept. Because you think of yourself as so high, if your shaykh says, "This one is your teacher," you must accept, finished! If you accept, you will not lose anything; instead, you will gain the power of *awlīyāullāh* and Prophet ﷺ because you accept what your shaykh is saying.

One day we passed through the very narrow alley that leads to Grandshaykh's house. Grandshaykh was in his room, and we heard him shouting and swearing, "You are (this), you are (that), I don't want to see your face!" We didn't dare move, afraid that Grandshaykh would shout at us, too!

Stupid people will look at that and speak badly about the person at whom the shaykh shouts. At the time there were five representatives of Grandshaykh ق and three of them attacked Mawlana Shaykh Nazim. Don't think everyone is going along nicely in this *ṭarīqah*; they are all attacking each other. If you look at the history of all the *ṭarīqahs*, after the shaykh passed away his representatives fought. Look at all the Islamic schools of thought, look at Muʿawiyah and ʿAli, or ʿAli and Aʿyesha, may Allāh be pleased with them all. May Allāh give Mawlana Shaykh long life because if he leaves, this *ṭarīqah* will split up into many branches, like a chicken, everyone wants to sit on their eggs, or like a rooster that can't sit on eggs but forces himself to sit anyway!

Everyone heard the shouting and we wanted to see who would come out. To our surprise, it was Mawlana Shaykh Nazim ق, smiling as if nothing had happened! Mawlana told us to go up to Grandshaykh, who was waiting for us and said, "Hisham, Adnan, come here!" We were trembling, thinking we would be next! He laughed and said, "*SubḥānAllāh*! No matter how much I shout at Nazim Effendi, nothing in his heart changes towards me."

When *awlīyā* say something, they check to see your reaction. The test was not with a normal one, but with someone who was with him for forty or fifty years. He was not shouting for Mawlana, but rather to see the reaction of others who heard it. They went against Mawlana Shaykh Nazim with such crudeness; one even hit him on his head with a *miswāk*! Grandshaykh ق said, "His heart never changed," and that's why he gave Mawlana Shaykh Nazim his *amānāt* and even more!

Once I went for Hajj with Mawlana, who took fifty elderly people with him. I said, "Mawlana, why are you taking these people?"

He replied, "I have to test my patience." All of them were elderly and some could not even move.

So we went, but there were no hotels, just homes with no toilets or running water. It was difficult, not like today. Mawlana wanted to convert some money. He asked a money-changer, who gave him an exchange rate, but Mawlana wanted to check for a better rate, so he asked another person, who did not give him not a good price.

Mawlana said, "The other one gave a better price."

The second one shouted, "I don't want to see you here! All of you foreigners are stupid and you come here and think you are something!" Then he collected all his saliva and spat on Mawlana! I rushed to beat him, but Mawlana stopped me and said, "Don't do anything." He wiped his face and was patient, because he knew Who is behind the one who moved that person to do that. If you don't believe that, you will never understand *ṭarīqah.*

May Allāh ﷻ forgive us and may Allāh ﷻ bless us.

Wa min Allāhi 't-tawfīq, bi ḥurmati 'l-ḥabīb, bi ḥurmati 'l-Fātiḥah.

And with Allāh is success. For the sake of the Beloved, for his sake we recite the opening chapter of Holy Qur'an.

Patience and Thankfulness, the Two Halves of Faith

Aʿūdhu billāhi min ash-Shayṭāni 'r-rajīm. Bismillāhi' r-Raḥmāni 'r-Raḥīm. Nawaytu 'l-arbāʿīn, nawaytu 'l-ʿitikāf, nawaytu'l-khalwah, nawaytu 'l-ʿuzlah, nawaytu 'r-riyāḍa, nawaytu 's-sulūk, lillāhi Taʿalā fī hādhā 'l-masjid. Atīʿūllāha wa atīʿū 'r-Rasūla wa ūli 'l-amri minkum. (4:59)

D*astūr yā Sayyidī, madad*! *Alḥamdūlillāh,* every day we are seeing new faces, not the same faces, but changing. That is a sign of Allāh's blessings on all of us. Allāh is sending His sincere servants. These associations are under Mawlana Shaykh Nazim's name and for anything under *awlīyāullāh's* name there is a special ocean from which *awlīyāullāh* drink and give to their followers. Every *walī* has a different ocean; not all *awlīyā* swim in the same ocean nor do they receive the same knowledge. In terms of Shariʿah all are the same, but Tazkiyyat an-Nafs, the Station of Purification of the Self, needs a lot of water from that ocean to clean the hearts of those who follow that shaykh.

When mining gold, they find gold along the rivers and wash away the sand to get the gold. Without the river they cannot get the gold. That flowing river is the heart of the *walī* from which anyone can quench their thirst and polish their heart from all kind of dirtiness and veils that block you from shining. There are veils between you and the Prophet ﷺ that block everything, and the shaykh is not blocked, but we are. As Grandshaykh ق said, "There are seventy thousand veils between us and the Prophet ﷺ, and if we don't remove them one by one, it will be impossible to reach our trust." Your trust can only be given in the presence of Prophet ﷺ; otherwise the shaykh cannot give it to you as it will not open.

So every *walī* swims in a different ocean, from which he gives his followers. Depending on the level of that *walī,* what you drink will become sweeter and sweeter. Some oceans are salty and some are sweet, like fresh-water rivers. Niagara Falls is like an ocean, but it is sweet. Depending on their levels, *awlīyāullāh* raise their students with them to drink from the ocean they are drinking from. They don't accept to have their followers drink from something else; all have to drink from the same place in order to quench their thirst according to that level of knowledge.

When he raises them and gives them to drink from that knowledge, from that Fountain of Youth, their hearts begin to shine like jewels, because the shaykh takes away the dirtiness with that ocean.

Allāh ﷻ said:

Wa jaʿalna min al-māʾi kulla shayʾin hayy.

We made from water every living thing. (Sūrat al-Anbīyā, 21:30)

Who Will Sit on the Heavenly Throne?

Many people translate this *āyah* as, "We have made from water everything alive." However, a *walī* does not read it like that; when he recites, *wa jaʿalna min al-māʾi kulla shayʾin hayy,* "We made from water every living thing," Prophet ﷺ dips him into the reality of that verse, where he sees all living things, *kulla shay,* everything! Who is this "everything?" Allāh ﷻ did not say, *baʿdu shayy,* "some things," as that might only indicate human beings, but rather, *kulla shayʾin hayy,* which means, "(We made from water) every living thing."

wa huwa 'Lladhī khalaqa 's-samāwāti wa 'l-arḍa fī sittati ayyāmin wa kāna ʿarshuhu ʿalā 'l-mā' li-yabluwakum ayyakum ahsanu ʿāmalā.

It is He who created the Heavens and the Earth in six days, and His Throne was upon the waters that He might try you, (and see) which of you excel in works. (Sūrat al-Hūd, 11:70)

Allāh ﷻ said His Throne was on water when He created Heavens and Earth in six days. What is that water? We don't know. While there is no time, place, or direction for Allāh ﷻ, He said, "His Throne was on water," indicating a place. There is a big exclamation mark here; what does that mean? We cannot open up that subject now as it is a very sensitive topic which *ʿulama* debate, concerning who will sit on the Holy Throne.

Allāh ﷻ said:

Ar-Raḥmān ʿalā 'l-ʿarsh istawā.

The Most Gracious is firmly established on the Throne (of authority).

(Sūrat al-TaHa, 20:5)

It is not "sitting," as many interpret it, but here "*istawā*" means "to take over," as in *Huwa ʿalā 'l-ʿarsh istawā,* "He took over the Throne." You cannot say Allāh ﷻ sits on the Throne as He does not sit on something He creates; He doesn't need to; rather, He "took it over." Then who will sit there?

Ibn Qayyim al-Jawziyya ؓ said in his book that Allāh will order Prophet ﷺ to sit on the Throne, and Sayyid Muḥammad ʿAlawi Maliki confirmed this in his book, Mafahim Yajib ʿan Tusahhah, "The Necessary Correction of Certain Misconceptions", stating: "Of course Prophet ﷺ will be sitting on the Throne if Allāh wills it. No one can say 'no' if Allāh says 'yes.'"

Ibn Qayyim al-Jawziyya was a student of Ibn Taymiyya and he wrote this in his book, and since he wrote it, if we can say he is the strongest proponent of the Salafi school of thought, Ibn Taymiyya, Ibn Katheer and others, if one of them confirmed that, why do Salafis object when Ahlu 's-Sunnah wa 'l-Jamaʿah praise the Prophet ﷺ? They have no right to object, because Allāh ﷻ is respecting and honoring His Prophet ﷺ, and also inviting him, as Ibn Qayyim said, "To sit on the Throne." This quote is authenticated by Sayyid Muḥammad ʿAlawi Maliki of Mecca, who included it in his book. So Salafis cannot legitimately run away from this belief as their scholars said it. This is evidence for them from their own books, and *awlīyāullāh* inherit these knowledges with its secrets.

"We made from water every living thing," but what is "every living thing?" Today they found the human body is comprised of 90-94% water. There is nothing in the universe that does not need water! So for the secret of existence and anything they want to know, *awlīyāullāh* take from that *āyah*. That is why when we read Qur'an we have to be careful to understand what we read, not to pass through it like a storyteller or someone reading a history book, or like a lecturer that quickly reviews. In every letter of Holy Qur'an there are 24,000 oceans of knowledge that will open to you! Everyone will have a different opening as Allāh ﷻ does not duplicate, so everyone will be given different knowledges; Allāh will give one something different from the other.

Therefore, we must have faith, which is why *imān* is the second religious category of Islam: *āmantu billāhi wa malā'ikatihi wa kutūbihi wa rusūlihi wa 'l-yawmi 'l-ākhir wa bi 'l-qadri khayrihi wa sharrihi min Allāhi Taʿala*, "I believe in Allāh, and His angels, and His books, and His messengers, and in the Last Day, and in Predestination good and bad, as ordained by Allāh, the Highest." *Imān* is important, as you must believe.

Three Elements of Knowledge: Islam, Iman and Ihsan

Islam is the base structure of the building, *imān* is its roof, and *ihsān* is the decoration. Islam consists of five pillars which you build in order to have the base structure. Then you need *imān,* belief, to build the roof, after which you will feel safe to enter and begin decorating with *ihsān,* moral excellence. So when you build Islam, *imān* and *ihsān* in your heart, and you will have a house decorated with Allāh's Beautiful Names and Attributes, as Prophet ﷺ said:

> *Qalb al-mu'min bayt ar-rabb.*
>
> *The heart of the believer is the House of Allāh.* (Ḥadīth Qudsī)

The House of Allāh ﷻ is decorated with *"lā ilāha illa-Llāh Muḥammadun Rasūlullāh,"* the decoration of the heart! The love for The Owner of that is the decoration of the heart. When you love Prophet ﷺ and read the Kalimat at-Tawhīd, you will be honored to receive the shining rainbow of Allāh's Beautiful Names and Attributes in your heart!

The Prophet ﷺ said:

> *Al-imān nisfān: nisfahu sabrun wa nisfun shukrun.*
>
> *Faith is of two halves: half is patience and half is being thankful.*

Imān is of two halves. If you are in *'ibādah,* worship, it means you believe in Allāh ﷻ. Your five daily prayers are considered worship, but you need *imān.* Some people in Arab countries or the Subcontinent were raised on prayer; they pray as a custom, but without belief. So you need *imān,* belief, and to have *imān* is to be patient on everything around you.

Be Patient, Make Peace and Forgive

Prophet ﷺ was the most patient on his *ummah.* An example of this is for seven years his neighbor dumped garbage on his doorstep but he never complained; he simply took the garbage and threw it away without telling anyone. The day his neighbor was about to die, Prophet ﷺ went to visit him. The neighbor was very surprised by this and said, "*Yā* Muḥammad! For seven years I threw garbage at your door, but you never said anything to me, I never heard you complain, and now you are coming to see me when I am dying? What kind of beautiful religion do you follow?"

So being patient with people's rudeness will one day attract them to you. Is it easy to be patient on someone who loves you, but to increase discipline, you must be patient on someone who harms you, then you will be a role model and people will become disciplined from the shining example of your behavior. You will learn from them and they will learn from you.

They asked a disciplined person, "Who taught you discipline?"

He said, "I learned discipline from those who have no discipline; I observed them and tried to avoid those behaviors until I became disciplined."

Imān makes us patient and forgiving. When you forgive Allāh ﷻ will reward you, as He mentioned in the Holy Qur'an:

Fa-man ʿafā wa aslaha fa-ajruhu ʿala-Llāhi innahu lā yuḥibbu 'ẓ-ẓālimīn.

Whosoever forgives and makes peace, his reward will be with Allāh. Surely, He does not love the cruel. (Sūrat ash-Shura, 42:40)

So if you want a reward from Allāh ﷻ, make peace and forgive those who harm you!

Once, while Sayyīdinā ʿUmar ؓ was in the presence of Prophet ﷺ, the Prophet ﷺ said, "That *Ṣaḥābī* will enter Paradise without giving an account." Sayyīdinā ʿUmar ؓ was happy to hear that and wanted to know more, so he went to that *Ṣaḥābī*'s home and knocked on his door. As soon as the *Ṣaḥābī* opened the door, he said, "O, Sayyīdinā ʿUmar! Please come in." Without asking him anything, he gave him food and a mattress to sleep on, because according to Arabic etiquette you must host your guests for three days without asking the reason of their visit. So after the three days were up, the host asked, "*Yā* ʿUmar! Is there anything you are requesting from me?"

Sayyīdinā ʿUmar ؓ said, "I'm wondering why the Prophet ﷺ said you will enter Paradise with no account when you are not doing anything special! I saw that we are doing more than you, as I was with you for three days. Tahajjud comes and you don't wake up, you only wake up for Fajr prayer while we are awake all night doing our Tahajjud prayers, then Maghrib comes and you don't pray Salātu 'l-Awwabīn or the other voluntary prayers what we do; like Salāt adh-Dhuha. So I don't understand why the Prophet ﷺ said that! Do you do something special?"

He said, "Yes, Sayyīdinā ʿUmar! Allāh ﷻ put three disciplines in my heart: first, before I go to sleep, I renew my creed by reciting the *shahādah,* the Kalimat at-Tawhīd. Every night before going to sleep, I must say, *'Ash-hadu an lā ilāha illa-Llāh, wa ash-hadu anna Muḥammadan Rasūlullāh.'"*

Don't only recite it, but contemplate it and feel as if you are in the Presence of Allāh ﷻ, saying, *"Ash-hadu an lā ilāha illa-Llāh, wa ash-hadu anna Muḥammadan Rasūlullāh."* Isn't it a nice feeling? You send yourself there; your soul can move and feel the presence, saying, *"Yā Rabbī! Ash-hadu an lā ilāha illa-Llāh, wa ash-hadu anna Muḥammadan Rasūlullāh!"* This will increase the Divine Presence within your heart. Day after day, that presence will become stronger and stronger until you begin to hear and see things.

That man continued, "Second, *yā* ʿUmar: in the morning, if *dunya* comes to me with all its treasures, it doesn't change me. I don't say I made millions and become happy as it doesn't mean anything to me! It is just dirty *dunya.* It is only useful for spending in the Way of Allāh ﷻ. In the evening, if I lose the whole *dunya* I don't get upset, I always say, '*Shukrān, yā Rabbī*!' And third, before I put my head on the pillow, I forgive everyone who has harmed me; I do not hold a drop of hatred against anyone."

Then Sayyīdinā ʿUmar ؓ said, "Now I understand why Prophet ﷺ said you are going to Paradise without giving any account."

Fa-man ʿafā wa aslaha fa-ajruhu ʿala-Llāh.

Whoever forgives and makes peace, his reward will be with Allāh.

(Sūrat ash-Shura, 42.40)

So that is the reward: to enter Paradise when you forgive! Allāh ﷻ is "The Forgiver," and when you forgive He is happy with you because He is saying, "I am The One Who forgives. Learn how to forgive people and I will forgive you on that difficult Day." Don't keep hatred for anyone in your heart; forgive them! Then Allāh ﷻ will make them forgive us also, as we are all falling into the traps of Shayṭān, hating this one or that one. When we forgive, Allāh forgives us!

So half of *imān* is to be patient. Being patient means you are someone who forgives, someone who doesn't carry hatred in his heart against anyone. The second half of *imān* is *ash-shukr*, to thank Allāh ﷻ, as He said:

Wa lā in shakartum la-azīdanakum.

If you thank Me, I will give you more. (Sūrat Ibrāhīm, 14:7)

Say, "*Shukrān, yā Allāh! Shukrān, yā Allāh!*" and Allāh ﷻ will give you more. But when there is too much *dunya* in our lives we forget to say, "*Shukrān, yā Rabbī,* thank you, O my Lord!" May Allāh ﷻ keep that *ḥadīth* in our hearts, to remember *imān* is of two halves, patience and thankfulness. If you balance that, all your deeds will be balanced.

One of Allāh's Beautiful Names and Attributes is "As-Sabūr, The Patient One." It is the Last Name of the Ninety-Nine Beautiful Names and it means, "I am the most patient on My servants." Is He not patient with us? Look at the ʿĀd, Thamūd and the people of Sayyīdinā Nuh ؏: Allāh ﷻ was not patient with them and destroyed them.

Wa qalīlan min ʿibādī ash-shakūr.

Only a few of My worshippers are thankful. (Sūrat Saba', 34:13)

Qalīl means "very few;" compared to billions it means nothing. So Allāh ﷻ says, "You must be within that few," who are thankful. If you are, *min ash-shākirīnullāh,* those who thank Allāh, then He will not put you down, He will lift you up. But we need faith, as without it neither patience nor thankfulness come; nothing comes, as faith brings everything!

The Prophet ﷺ said:

Al-ʿulama warithatu 'l-anbīyā.

The (genuine) scholars are the inheritors of prophets.

Those who are here will listen and for those who are not here, Mawlana's *suḥbah* reaches the heart of every *murīd,* wherever they are! When you are authorized to speak, it must reach the heart of everyone who took the hand of Mawlana Shaykh Nazim ق.

May Allāh ﷻ forgive us and may Allāh ﷻ bless us.

Wa min Allāhi 't-tawfīq, bi ḥurmati 'l-ḥabīb, bi ḥurmati 'l-Fātiḥah.
And with Allāh is success. For the sake of the Beloved, for his sake we recite the opening chapter of Holy Qur'an.

The Power of Presenting Our Dhikr to Shah Naqshband

A'ūdhu billāhi min ash-Shayṭāni 'r-rajīm. Bismillāhi' r-Raḥmāni 'r-Raḥīm. Nawaytu 'l-arbā'īn, nawaytu 'l-'itikāf, nawaytu'l-khalwah, nawaytu 'l-'uzlah, nawaytu 'r-riyāḍa, nawaytu 's-sulūk, lillāhi Ta'alā fī hādhā 'l-masjid. Atī'ūllāha wa atī'ū 'r-Rasūla wa ūli 'l-amri minkum. (4:59)

There is a secret in the universe: "Obey Allāh, obey the Prophet and obey those in authority among you." Grandshaykh ق and Mawlana Shaykh Nazim, may Allāh give him long life, said, "Anyone who recites that verse, when he says *'atī'ūllāh,* obey Allāh,' it will be as if he performed all his obligations and stopped committing forbiddens." That is a secret! Allāh's Words are not like ours; our words are limited in meaning, but Allāh's Words never end, as He said in the Holy Qur'an:

> *Qul law kāna 'l-baḥru midādan li-kalimāti Rabbī la-nafida 'l-baḥru qabla an tanfada kalimātu Rabbī wa law ji'nā bi-mithlihi madada.*
>
> *Say (O Muḥammad), "And if the oceans were ink and the trees pens, they would be used up before writing the Words of our Lord even if we added another ocean like it, for its aid."* (Sūrat al-Kahf, 18:109)

If trees were pens and oceans were ink, first the wood would dissolve and the ink would finish as Allāh's words will never end! There are around 300,000 words in the Holy Qur'an which, if you write them all they will finish, but here Allāh ﷻ is saying, "It doesn't finish; only in your knowledge it is finished." For example, if you read one *juz* of Holy Qur'an every day you will complete a full reading in thirty days; however, Allāh ﷻ is saying it doesn't finish because the words have secrets. You may understand one meaning of a word, but that is not all the meanings. No one can swim in the ocean of Holy Qur'an and say it will finish, because Allāh's Ocean of Words will never end. This shows that there are meanings behind every letter in a word, and there are around 600,000 letters in the Holy Qur'an!

Grandshaykh 'Abd-Allāh al-Fa'iz ad-Daghestāni ق said, "For every letter of the Holy Qur'an, Allāh ﷻ opened 24,000 oceans of knowledge to His *awlīyāullāh,* and what He opened to one *walī* He did not open to another as He doesn't duplicate, and all of Allāh's Words are within the *āyah, ati'ullāha wa ati'u 'r-Rasūla wa ūli 'l-amri minkum,* "Obey Allāh, obey the Prophet, and obey those in authority among you."

The Prophet ﷺ said:

YaSīn qalb al-qur'an.

(Surah) YaSīn is the heart of Qur'an. (al-Tirmidhi)

That means Muḥammad ﷺ is the heart of Qur'an as "YaSīn" is Muḥammad ﷺ! Also, Allāh ﷻ said:

YaSīn wal qur'ani 'l-hakīm.

YaSīn and the wise Qur'an. (Sūrat al-YaSīn, 36:1-2)

By saying, "YaSīn and the Qur'an," Allāh is making *'ataf,* putting one sentence over the other. Allāh ﷻ gave greatness to Prophet ﷺ here, as it is, "him ﷺ and the Holy Qur'an!" That's why, it is said that "YaSīn," meaning Sayyīdinā Muḥammad, is the heart of Qur'an and al-Fātiḥah is the heart of Muḥammad ﷺ! If you don't recite the seven verses of Sūrat al-Fātiḥah in your prayer, it is not accepted. If you recite Sūrat al-Fātiḥah alone, with no *āyah* or *sūrah* after, your prayer will still be valid, but not without it. This means your prayer is accepted when you acknowledge/ include "the heart of Prophet ﷺ," which is always radiant in every prayer.

So when Allāh ﷻ says, "My Words never end," it means for every word of Holy Qur'an there are endless interpretations and secrets. So if you add all *awlīyāullāh*'s knowledge from the time of Sayyīdinā Abū Bakr ؓ, Sayyīdinā 'Umar ؓ, Sayyīdinā Uthmān ؓ, Sayyīdinā 'Ali ؓ, and all *awlīyāullāh* up to Mawlana Shaykh Nazim ق, including all branches of the Naqshbandi Order and other *ṭarīqahs,* and all the 124,000 *awlīyāullāh,* of which 7007 are Naqshbandi and the rest are from different *ṭarīqahs,* it would not come to the meaning of a single word in the Holy Qur'an!

There are many *awlīyāullāh,* but not all are on the same highway. In spirituality, there is discipline. Every *walī* is on his own highway with his followers, so don't jump from one *walī* to another! All are taking from the Prophet ﷺ as it is said, *wa kullu min rasūlullāh multamisan,* "All are taking from that flow of knowledge coming from Prophet ﷺ."

Even with all that accumulated knowledge they will still not say, "We know," because there is yet more! For example, if you go to a bookstore and search for books on Islamic spirituality, you can find thousands of books from all around the world, and if all of these were put together, it would not be a drop of that ocean, as Grandshaykh ق and Mawlana Shaykh Nazim ق said, "Only Allāh knows whatever knowledge Allāh ﷻ gave to Prophet ﷺ." It is not but one drop of the knowledge He is giving to Prophet ﷺ in every moment! The Holy Qur'an is the Word of Allāh ﷻ, so no one can truly understand it as that complete knowledge is only for Prophet ﷺ and *awlīyāullāh* can only know what is given to their hearts by Prophet ﷺ, not more. They stand at the shore of the Ocean of Knowledge, the Ocean of Prophet ﷺ, *hayāran*, stunned and astonished.

The Challenge of Sayyidina Bayazid al-Bistami

Grandshaykh ق told us that once Sayyīdinā Abū Yazīd al-Bistāmi ق was in the association of *awlīyāullāh*. Some *awlīyāullāh* remain in the presence of Prophet ﷺ, and some are given one minute, or one or two hours in that presence, depending on how much they can receive. In the association of the grand *awlīyāullāh* with Prophet ﷺ and the *Ṣaḥābah* ﷺ, with permission of Prophet ﷺ, Sayyīdinā Abū Yazīd al-Bistāmi ق addressed all the *awlīyā*.

What we are speaking of is a spiritual vision, *kashf*, as mentioned in the *ḥadīth* of Prophet ﷺ, when Allāh ﷻ said:

> *My servant does not cease to approach Me through voluntary worship until I will love him. When I love him, I will become the ears with which he hears, the eyes with which he sees the hand with which he acts, and the legs with which he walks (and other versions include, "and the tongue with which he speaks.")*
>
> (Ḥadīth Qudsī, Bukhāri)

Awlīyāullāh can see with the light Allāh ﷻ gave them. So in that *kashf*, Sayyīdinā Abū Yazīd al-Bistāmi ق said, "I have a comment." *Awlīyāullāh* can complain or make comments, but not all of them do, as some choose to surrender and don't say anything; they listen, and when an order comes from Prophet ﷺ they follow it. He said, "When all the *murīds* of the Naqshbandi Ṭarīqah perform the Ihda, "Why do they say, '*khāssatan*, especially to Shah Naqshband?' If they give me that Ihda and say, 'especially to Bayazīd al-Bistāmi,' I will put them on the shore of that ocean, as I have the power!"

Look how strong that Ihda is! They carry you to the shore of the Ocean of Knowledge, where Prophet ﷺ is! Abū Yazīd al-Bistāmi ق said, "If they say, *'ila ruhi imāmi-t-ṭarīqah wa ghawthi 'l-khaliqat Bayazīd al-Bistāmi,* 'Grant the reward of what we have read in particular to the soul of the *imām* of the *ṭarīqah* and arch-Intercessor of the created world, Bayazīd al-Bistāmi,' I will take them to that shore where no one can reach, where I am standing, waiting for them!"

Then one *walī* asked permission to speak in the spiritual presence of Prophet ﷺ; I have no permission to mention his name, but he said, *"Yā Sayyidī, yā Bayazīd!* Yes, you can put them on that shore, but you are saying this because you are not seeing Shah Naqshband on the other side of that shore. Of course if someone is not there, how can he put his *murīds* there? But Shah Bahauddin Naqshband is already on the other shore, putting them all there! With the Prophet's blessings, he crossed that ocean of sainthood and placed his *murīds* on the other side, where they are 'ready-made' Naqshbandis—ready, as if that whole ocean had been poured into their hearts!"

This is the case every time you read the Ihda! Sayyīdinā Shah Naqshband ق and *awlīyāullāh* are able to take their followers to where they are, and not every *walī* can do this, as it is a specialty Allāh ﷻ gives to some of His *awlīyāullāh.* With all our respect to *awlīyāullāh,* this is how it works. Some of them have been chosen to speak, like Sayyīdinā Bayazīd al-Bistāmi, who made lots of *da'wah.* Some *awlīyā* don't speak; you sit with them, they make *dhikr* and that's it, but they might be stronger.

One of the grandshaykhs of the Naqshbandi Ṭarīqah, Sayyīdinā Abū Aḥmad as-Sughuri ق said, "If I had the tongue of Sayyīdinā Jamaluddīn al-Ghumuqi al-Husayni ق, I could have made everyone Muslim!" This means, he was not given permission to bring out knowledge from the heart to the tongue. If that is for the tongue, then what do you think is in the heart? They have many things to say, but they are not allowed. From one *walī* to another power will increase. That is not to humiliate the other *awlīyāullāh,* but this is how it works, because in every moment Prophet ﷺ is in ascension and many different knowledges come.

The Holy Ascension Is Continuous and Impacts Us

In *fiqh,* Islamic jurisprudence, Prophet ﷺ relates a *ḥadīth,* but after a few days or week he relates the same *ḥadīth* in a different way, because when he is in ascension he relates that same *ḥadīth* from the different levels he is in, so it changes. Similarly, there are changes according to the ascensions of *awlīyāullāh*; they change whatever they see or are ordered to do, whether you like it or not. So we have to say, *samiʿna wa ataʿna,* "We hear and we obey." You cannot say, "I heard it, but I don't want to obey." You must obey and accept; if you accept, you might be raised higher because their words are tests for everyone and there are many hidden things in their words.

That *walī* said, "Shah Naqshband is putting them on the other shore." This means, Shah Naqshband ق is taking all these secrets Allāh ﷻ is giving him from one shore to another! Sayyīdinā Bayazīd al-Bistāmi ق took these secrets to his shore, then from his shore to the second begins all the other shores of *awlīyāullāh* until they come to Shah Naqshband ق. What then do you think of Grandshaykh ʿAbdAllāh al-Fa'iz ad-Daghestāni ق, as all these secrets have come to him, and now to Mawlana Shaykh Nazim ق!

Everything is in ascension. We are also in ascension, as our hearts are constantly being uploaded with new knowledge, but you need a password. Today, they cannot open something without a password. *Awlīyāullāh* are always uploading and giving, even if you are not sitting with them, as Prophet ﷺ said:

Lī saʿatun maʿ Allāh wa saʿatun maʿ al-khalq.

I have one hour in the Divine Presence and one hour with the Creation.

In another *ḥadīth* that differs slightly, he ﷺ also said:

Lī wajhun maʿ Allāh wa wajhun maʿ al-khalq.

I have one face in the Divine Presence and one face with the Creation.

So *awlīyāullāh* are inheriting these secrets from the Prophet ﷺ and they are with their followers, regardless of what the followers do. Even if the *murīd* is at a disco, they can reach him and upload to his heart and they will never stop uploading because they know one day he will return to his senses, repent, and come to find all those knowledges waiting for him, because he extended his hand to his shaykh to take *baya'*.

That *bayaʿ* is connected, so he is chained! They let you go as much as you like, even if you don't come back, because eventually on the last seven breaths you will come back, as they will be present with you. Many *murīds* leave their promise or contract with their shaykh, but they cannot change what has been written, that they will be with that *walī*. Even if they leave the *walī* and go back to *dunya,* they are still under his name. But if someone is lazy, what can we do?

Allah's Words and Their Secrets Never End

So that is how they are able to reach and upload to your heart, but with what? That ocean is full of knowledge because *awlīyāullāh* are taking from the words of Holy Qur'an. Oceans will finish, but Allāh's Word will never finish, which means the secrets of the words will never finish; one word from Holy Qur'an can drown the whole universe, which is not even a drop in the ocean of that word! Allāh ﷻ is al-Khaliq, "The Creator (Who creates in every moment with no limits)," and al-ʿĀlim, "The Knower." You cannot limit the Greatness of Allāh ﷻ; it is unlimited! As soon as He wills to create, creation occurs in every moment with no limits, and there is no way of knowing its beginning or its end.

This universe is moving in space. To give an example, we will go along with what the scientists say, that since the 'Big Bang' billions of years have passed, but it is not as they say for we have many proofs that refute it. Since then this whole universe, with its 6000 galaxies each consisting of 80 billion stars, is moving in a vacuum at a speed of 300,000 km per second, non-stop up to this moment. No one knows where it is moving as there is no direction in space. How is this universe moving in a vacuum with no air, while here on this small planet there is air for us to breath? Look at Allāh's Greatness! Allāh ﷻ wants to show you, "On the smallest planet I created, I gave all this life. O human beings! Don't you think that I have other Creations much bigger and much greater?"

Allāh ﷻ made all of that to be under the authority of Prophet ﷺ. Do you see the greatness of the Prophet ﷺ? So in every moment, the Greatness of the Creator, al-Khaliq, is shown through His Creation, and we didn't speak of angels yet. The creation of angels is not like the creation of human beings in that we have limited reproduction capability, but their capability is unlimited. Allāh creates angels in every moment that are completely different from the ones before; they neither look alike nor do they make the same *taṣbīh*. Their *ḥamd, tahlīl, takbīr,* and *taṣbīh* are entirely different from any other angel, as all are different.

The angels of glorification will never repeat the same *taṣbīh;* for example, if the same angel says "*subḥān-Allāh,*" the next moment he might say, "*Allāhu Akbar.*" Allāh knows what words He gives them to recite, like words in Holy Qur'an that no one knows their meaning: *"Alif. Lām. Mīm," "Qāf. Hā. Yā. ʿAyn. Sād," "Hā. Mīm. ʿAyn. Sīn. Qāf,"* and so on.

So the guidance of *shuyūkh* is important, because they encourage you to have more love for Allāh ﷻ, for His Prophet ﷺ, and for your guide. That is why all knowledges are embedded in that *āyah*:

Atīʿūllāha wa atīʿū 'r-Rasūla wa ūli 'l-amri minkum.

Obey Allāh, obey the Prophet, and obey those in authority among you.

(Sūrat an-Nisa, 4:59)

If you recite this verse one-hundred times a day, you will benefit, as if you worshipped Allāh ﷻ every day with complete *iʿtāt*, obedience to Him and to His Prophet ﷺ! May Allāh forgive us and bless this association. We thank everyone who came here. This place is for everyone.

May Allāh ﷻ give Mawlana Shaykh Nazim al-Haqqani long life and give all of you long life.

May Allāh ﷻ forgive us and may Allāh ﷻ bless us.

Wa min Allāhi 't-tawfiq, bi ḥurmati 'l-ḥabīb, bi ḥurmati 'l-Fātiḥah.

And with Allāh is success. For the sake of the Beloved, for his sake we recite the opening chapter of Holy Qur'an.

Patience During Affliction Is Essential

A'ūdhu billāhi min ash-Shayṭāni 'r-rajīm. Bismillāhi' r-Raḥmāni 'r-Raḥīm. Nawaytu 'l-arbā'īn, nawaytu 'l-'itikāf, nawaytu'l-khalwah, nawaytu 'l-'uzlah, nawaytu 'r-riyāḍa, nawaytu 's-sulūk, lillāhi Ta'alā fī hādhā 'l-masjid. Atī'ūllāha wa atī'ū 'r-Rasūla wa ūli 'l-amri minkum. (4:59)

School begins with kindergarten, then intermediate grades, then on to high school, then college or university, then a post-graduate program, then some go on to a PhD program. At the lower level you are hired, and after teaching for ten years you may become an associate professor and later, a full professor. The career progresses gradually.

Also we give an analogy that you need to capture the moments in which Allāh's Beautiful Names and Attributes are manifest, and then you reach the peak and find yourself in the presence of Prophet ﷺ. Similarly, if you don't reach there, blame yourself and not your teacher, who said, "Come! Our doors are open from east to west." When you come in they close the doors, there is no exit, but come anyway. They close the door in order that Shayṭān will not steal from you any of these moments which are important in our spiritual journey. So when we are not in that presence we know we are helpless and weak, and we cannot achieve what they want us to achieve. That is why *awlīyāullāh* guide us from their generosity and their own experience.

It is said, "Spend whatever is in your pocket and Allāh will repay it from His Own treasures." *Awlīyāullāh* are so generous that they spend on their followers whatever they acquired, not only money, but whatever Allāh ﷻ gave them. They do not allow their followers to remain dirty; rather, they carry them, give to them, and they dutifully wait for Allāh to send more, because Allāh ﷻ said *ḥasanāt* will be multiplied by ten. For any good you do in accordance with Shari'ah and *ṭarīqah,* Allāh ﷻ will reward you tenfold, and *awlīyāullāh* love to share that with their students.

Allāhu Akbar! For you, one *ḥasanāh* becomes ten, but for struggling in the way of Allāh ﷻ and Prophet ﷺ, Allāh gives you the reward of seventy martyrs! You get more when you struggle to revive the *sunnah* of Prophet ﷺ, as Allāh loves His servants to follow in the footsteps of His Beloved! If you struggle to achieve something for yourself, you get ten rewards, but if you do it for Allāh and the Prophet ﷺ, you get the reward of seventy martyrs. *Allāhu Akbar*!

Allāh ﷻ knows what kind of rewards you get. Martyrs are alive in Barzakh and provided with all heavenly manifestations. You will get what they get simply by reviving one *sunnah*! That is why it is recommended to wear a ring, a turban, or to carry a stick, *sunnat* that are easy to fulfill, but there are *sunnat* that are difficult to fulfill and no one can do them:

Yā ayyuha 'l-muzzammil, qumi 'l-layl illa qalīla, nisfahu awi 'nqus minhu qalīla, aw zid ʿalayhi wa rattili 'l-qur'ana tartīla.

O thou, wrapped in garments! Stand (in prayer) by night, but not all night, of one-half thereof or less, or add to it (at will), and recite the Qur'an calmly and distinctly, with your mind attuned to its meaning.

(Sūrat al-Muzzammil, 73:1-4)

Allāh ﷻ said this to Prophet ﷺ for us to learn. The literal meaning is, "O Muḥammad, you are covered! Wake up. Stand up for Allāh ﷻ for most of the night, but never mind, We know you get tired, so stand up for half of it or less." Who can do that? In Ramaḍān you are forced to do that, but if not for Ramaḍān you would never do it! *SubḥānAllāh,* everything changes because the *tajalli* of Ramaḍān is different, everything is changed, and you are a little tired but can keep up with the extra obligations and fasting. What do you think when Allāh ﷻ is asking Prophet ﷺ to wake up night after night, with no holidays, because he is in the Presence of Allāh ﷻ? That is why Prophet ﷺ is happy to be in prayer!

We are blind, but if we were to follow this way we would see it. *Awlīyāullāh* did not stop, they said, "We will keep going," and although they might be tested a lot, they kept struggling and they reached the door. We have to struggle and keep going, but because we are lazy we cannot reach that door, so we ask Allāh ﷻ for the sake of Prophet ﷺ, "Bless us with that *tajalli,* to be in the presence of Prophet ﷺ! We are weak servants, we are not *awlīyāullāh* and we can't do what they do, but help us! You can support us because our intention is good."

Surety that Allah Rewards Tenfold

So we have to get that *barakah,* for every *ḥasanāh* you get ten rewards. If a *walī* gives one, he gets ten more; he knows that he is not losing. He gives physically and spiritually, but his pockets are never empty. Here are some examples.

A destitute lady came to the door of Sayyida Aʿyesha ﷺ and asked, "*Yā* Aʿyesha, please give us from what Allāh gave you." She had only three dates that she was saving for the Seal of Messengers ﷺ, who tied a stone on his stomach to stave off hunger, while if we don't see kabobs every day we are unhappy! So Sayyida Aʿyesha ﷺ gave the three dates to that lady, who gave one each to her two daughters and they ate them quickly. The situation was the same as in Somalia, where every day 12,000 people are dying; it is a humanitarian disaster. The lady took the third date from her mouth and shared half with each child. Prophet ﷺ said to Aʿyesha, "This lady will enter Paradise." That *barakah* is from one date!

One person who was walking in the desert was extremely thirsty and had nothing to eat. Finally, he reached a well preserved for travelers. He went into the well and quenched his thirst. When he finished, he went back up, where he saw a thirsty dog that could not go down the well to fetch water, so the man took off his *khuff* (leather sock), filled it with water, and gave it to the dog to drink. When the dog finished he went on his way, happy. Prophet ﷺ said, "That man will go to Paradise for that kindness."

When you give, Allāh ﷻ gives back to you, but don't think whatever you give, for example, one million pounds, will get ten million back, because each *ḥasanāh* is rewarded ten times. Therefore, Allāh may save you from cancer or a car accident. Which is worth more, ten million pounds or your life? Don't think you didn't get your charity back tenfold!

Once someone came to the door of a *walī* and asked for food. That *walī* had ten eggs and told his servant to give the hungry person all ten eggs. The servant decided to give him nine eggs and save one, thinking, "My master will break fast at Maghrib, so I will save one for him." She was not saving for herself, but thinking of the master. Where can you find that now? A husband doesn't save anything for his wife, nor a wife for her husband, and then they quarrel.

In the evening, there was a knock at the door. The servant opened the door and a stranger said, "Give this basket of eggs to your master as our gift." She was very happy and ran to the master, saying, "One person whom I don't know gave you these eggs."

He said, "Count them." She counted ninety eggs. He said, "I don't understand, why there are ninety eggs, why not one-hundred?"

"From the ten, I saved one for you," she replied.

He said, "You saved one egg and made us lose ten."

Allāh ﷻ will give you ten rewards for one *ḥasanāh.* This is how they were in relationship to their Lord. They believed Allāh will give and that He never withholds His generosity from anyone, but your *ʿamal* may delay what He gives. If there is a hole in your basket, mend it!

Reach Realities with Discipline and Obedience

At that time they believed in everything in the Holy Qur'an and thus, they were rewarded. Today we believe in Facebook, Twitter, Google, and Yahoo. Do you check on the Internet for anything else? Before, they used to check with their heavenly computer what Allāh gave their hearts, the six "Realities of Existence," which we all have: *Ḥaqīqatu 'l-Jazbah, Ḥaqīqatu 'l-Fayd, Ḥaqīqatu 't-Tawajah, Ḥaqīqatu 't-Tawassul, Ḥaqīqatu 'l-Irshād,* and *Ḥaqīqatu 't-Taʿī.*

For example, in the state of *Ḥaqīqat al-Jazbah,* the Reality of Attraction, you can attract heavenly manifestations, *ṣalāt ʿalā 'n-Nabī* ﷺ, *maʿrifatullāh,* people, and more.

In *Ḥaqīqat al-Fayd,* manifestations of the "Reality of the Beautiful Names and Attributes" are present in your heart; it is closed, but you can retrieve it.

Ḥaqīqat at-Tawajjuh is telepathy. An example is when Sayyīdinā 'Umar ؓ spoke to Sariah in Syria in a 3-D color picture, not flat like a TV image. He was seeing and hearing, but Sariah was only hearing as he was not at the level of Sayyīdinā 'Umar. They did not do anything wrong against Holy Qur'an and *sunnah.* Their relationship with their Lord was that of love, respect, and obedience.

When you know the discipline and are obedient then they let you in, the doors are open. There are bodyguards who check you first to see if you are up to their standard, and if not, they do not let you in. There are heavenly security guards (angels) at the door of Paradise who check if you have any sins. If you do, they ask you to take a shower and come back, they don't say "no." The door is always open, but there is a doorkeeper. If you are not in good condition, go clean yourself and return. It is not like *dunya* where they say, "Okay, go to prison." Allāh ﷻ does not send you to prison; rather, He says, "Fix yourself and come again."

Again, we quote from the book Talkhīs al-Ma'ārif, "Summarizing the Knowledges":

> O my brothers! Leave that craziness in your mind and follow the sincere ones in what they say and how they act. It is not only what they say, they must also act accordingly; otherwise, they will become charlatans (who use religion and spirituality for their own benefit). What is the benefit if they are not practicing? Don't ask to reach what they have reached by false claims, but say what you really are: a weak servant full of sins! Don't claim that you are like them or you will receive from them when your actions are not according to their teaching. If you wish to reach where they reached, you must be patient during *bala*, affliction. That is the door to Paradise, because when Allāh ﷻ sends afflictions and you continue on your path without looking here and there, you reach that door.
>
> Do not fight with people for certain issues. If someone wants to fight say, "I don't want to fight." It is better to say, "I am sorry, my brother. You are right," and Allāh will be more happy with you. Be patient during afflictions just as *awlīyāullāh* have waited, and keep going until you reach where they reached.

It is not that easy or cheap to reach that door! Even if you have a turban the size of a large tray of sweets, still you are not going to reach, so it is better to show humility.

> *Law lā 'l-bala la-kana 'n-nāsū kullun 'ubbādan zuhādan.*
>
> *If there were no afflictions on Earth, the Earth would be Paradise and all human beings would be in a state of asceticism.*
>
> (Shaykh Abd al-Qadir Jilani, al-Fath al-Rabbānī wal-Fayd al-Rahmāni)

There they would not care for *dunya* and would always want to be in the Divine Presence.

Afflictions make you go backward. If you lose your patience and get angry, more veils will cover your heart. So don't say, "I have been in *ṭarīqah* for thirty years and I haven't seen anything yet." Are you patient during affliction? Allāh sent that to check you!

Prophet ﷺ said, "I was the most abused and tortured by my relatives." Then where do we stand when, if we are tortured just a little bit, we go crazy? "Whoever is not patient will not receive *'atā-Allāh.*" Allāh ﷻ wants you to have patience. Sayyīdinā Adam ﷺ was patient; he went into *sajda* for forty years and never raised his head until Allāh ﷻ said, "You are forgiven." On the other hand, Iblīs was impatient and immediately complained, "You made me commit a sin!" Adam ﷺ didn't say anything and immediately went into *sajda* to seek Allāh's forgiveness.

If we face a problem, do we immediately go into *sajda*? Instead, we will use a gun to settle the matter! "If you discard patience then you were not patient on patience and you did not accept, and you closed the door of *ridā-Allāh*. Then you will be under a big question mark for abandoning servanthood." At that time you will not be a servant to Allāh ﷻ, but a servant to Shayṭān!

Prophet ﷺ said that Allāh ﷻ said:

Man lā yardā bi qadāī wa lam yasbir ʿalā balāī fa 'l-yattikhadh rabban siwā'ī.

Whoever does not accept My Will on him and is not patient on the affliction I send on him, let him find another God. (Ibn Asakir, Ḥadīth Qudsī)

So you have a choice: either accept and be blessed by Allāh ﷻ, or reject and leave this way to go to Shayṭān! *Awlīyāullāh* are showing us the way to accept struggles and have patience for the sake of Prophet ﷺ, to cure our mistakes. May Allāh ﷻ give us patience for the sake of His Prophet ﷺ.

May Allāh ﷻ forgive us and may Allāh ﷻ bless us.

Wa min Allāhi ʿt-tawfīq, bi ḥurmati ʿl-ḥabīb, bi ḥurmati ʿl-Fātiḥah.

And with Allāh is success. For the sake of the Beloved, for his sake we recite the opening chapter of Holy Qur'an.

The Believer Is the Mirror of His Brother

A'ūdhu billāhi min ash-Shayṭāni 'r-rajīm. Bismillāhi' r-Raḥmāni 'r-Raḥīm. Nawaytu 'l-arbā'īn, nawaytu 'l-'itikāf, nawaytu'l-khalwah, nawaytu 'l-'uzlah, nawaytu 'r-riyāḍa, nawaytu 's-sulūk, lillāhi Ta'alā fi hādhā 'l-masjid. Atī'ūllāha wa atī'ū 'r-Rasūla wa ūli 'l-amri minkum. (4:59)

Like all these decorations on the wall, the Prophet ﷺ said, *ad-dīnu nasīha,* "Religion is advice." Without advice, you cannot decorate your heart. Advice from those to whom Allāh ﷻ gave authority over us is like beautifully framed art. In order to make your *masjid* nice you put up '*Asmā'ullāh al-Husna* or '*Asma an-Nabī* ﷺ or calligraphy of verses of Holy Qur'an. That is for a *masjid,* where you cannot do anything except *'ibādah,* worship—not review tactics or find work or plan for *dunya,* because in a *masjid* only *'ibādah* is permitted.

The heart of the believer is the same. As the Prophet ﷺ said, "The heart of a believer is the House of Allāh." So look how they decorated Ka'batullāh from the outside, although it is already decorated with *Asmā'ullāh al-Husna.* With the Light of the Beautiful Names and Attributes Allāh ﷻ is sending on it, it is already decorated! So our job is to decorate our hearts with Allāh's Light; otherwise, dark veils will drop on us, then another and another until you cannot see any more. You will realize that whatever you do will go astray because all you see is darkness.

How Veils Are Lifted in Naqshbandi Tariqah

Between us and Sayyīdinā Muḥammad ﷺ there are 70,000 veils! People recite, *"Naray takbīr, naray Risalah."* When you say, *"Naray takbīr,"* you must see that Light within your heart, and when you say, *"Naray Risalah"* you must see the Prophet ﷺ in your heart. If not, then your recitations are only artificial. Our duty is to implement our knowledge of Allāh ﷻ, *ma'rifatullāh,* to take us to the light of the heart. Throw those veils out and the light of the heart will appear! If you close the curtains in this room and turn on the light, this room will still appear dark to someone outside. Similarly, there are veils that block light of the heart, so you must eliminate them.

In the Naqshbandi Order there are 70,000 veils. Our problem is that we have very thick veils and the thickest veil for everyone is *"Maqām al-'Awwām."* The first veil is thick, making it impossible to see. If that veil is taken away you see everything. This is the way of Naqshbandi Ṭarīqah, and especially in the Daghestāni branch that comes from the Prophet ﷺ to Sayyīdinā Abū Bakr ق, to Sayyīdinā Jaʿfar as-Sadiq ق, merging from Sayyīdinā ʿAli ق and Sayyīdinā Abū Bakr ؓ, then going all the way to Daghestan and Khas Muḥammad ق, to Sayyid Jamaluddin ق, then to Grandshaykh ʿAbdAllāh al-Faʾiz ad-Daghestāni ق and to Mawlana Shaykh Muḥammad Nazim al-Haqqani ق. They don't remove the thick veil.

In other *ṭarīqahs* they take the first veil away, then the second, then the third, the fourth, and you begin to see. As the veils are less thick, it becomes lighter and lighter so you are able to see and you are happy, saying, "*Allāhu Akbar!* This is the best *ṭarīqah*. I am progressing!" The veils are taken away, one by one, one by one, and then you come to a state in which you are so happy and thrilled and you are not able to progress any further because you find happiness in that level.

In Naqshbandi Ṭarīqah they don't do that, they begin from the back. They take away the lightest, the next lightest, then the next lightest, and so on, but the thick veil is intact, so you cannot see you are improving. In reality, you are improving but they don't want you to be busy on that level, showing miracles and saying, "I know the future," and so on. In the Naqshbandi Order they don't show miracles! In the Golden Chain they say, "Divorce miracles," not three times, but six times! And they say, "If a miracle comes to you, leave it." That is why they don't perform miracles in a direct way, only in indirect ways (that deflect attention from them).

In other *ṭarīqahs*, because the thick veil is taken away first, disciples begin to see something and they reveal it. In the Naqshbandi Order, *awlīyāullāh* keep the thick veil intact until they are very sure you are ready. When the Prophet ﷺ gives permission, they take the final veil and you find yourself in the presence of the Prophet ﷺ! That is the specialty of the Naqshbandi Order: as much as you polish your heart, you are able to see more and more in the presence of the Prophet ﷺ and knowledge comes to you.

That is why the Prophet ﷺ said:

Al-muʾmin mirāta akhīhi.

The believer is the mirror of his brother.

Why You Need a Mirror

The heart becomes a mirror in which your brother/sister sees himself/herself. As you became a mirror, good characteristics in your heart reflect on him when he looks in that mirror. That is why in the time of Imām al-Mahdi ﷺ you will not read books; they will all be burned until only the Holy Qur'an will remain. Also, any Qur'an not written in saffron will be burned, because today they print books with ink and a chemical by-product of urine that strengthens it from fading.

That will not be allowed in the time of al-Mahdi ﷺ; only pure ones will be allowed and only pure manuscripts will remain. Also in his time, knowledge will be given through the reflection of eyes from the one who received the knowledge to your eyes and heart, then you will reflect to another, he to another, and so on. They never knew that the meaning of "The *mu'min* is a mirror to his brother," applies to al-Mahdi's time!

In a previous time there was a king who wanted to make an artistic competition between the best painters of the day. They eliminated competitors one after another until the two best remained, and they took them to a place where they could paint a mural. They put each artist on opposite sides of a huge wall and each mural was covered by a curtain, so the artists could not influence one another and their paintings remained secret. One began to paint very nicely and the other began to polish the wall, cleaning it. Before the judging, the king wanted to see what they had done, so they opened the curtains to see both paintings. On one he saw very exquisite calligraphy. On the other there was nothing.

He asked the second artist, "What are you doing?"

He said, "I am polishing the wall. Please don't ask me."

So the day came and they went to see who had won. They opened the curtain, and for the first artist the painting was nice and the king was very happy. Then they looked at the second one and the painting was so nice because his wall had become a high-quality mirror; you could not see which mural was the original. Hence, "The *mu'min* is the mirror of his brother."

Once Sayyida 'Ayesha ؓ was not happy about the Prophet ﷺ going to a *masjid* in his best appearance, grooming his beard and wearing nice clothes. She said, "Yā Rasūlullāh! Where are you going?" He ﷺ replied, "Umm al-Mu'minīn! I am going to the *masjid*."

Lī wajhun maʿ al-khāliq wa wajhun maʿ al-khalq.
I have one face with people and one with the Creator.

Sayyida ʿAyesha ﷺ said, "No, you are going somewhere else," and that made the Prophet ﷺ unhappy. Then her father, Sayyīdinā Abū Bakr ﷺ slapped her, which also made the Prophet ﷺ unhappy. He said, "*Yā* Abū Bakr, don't do that anymore. I am a mirror; you looked at me and saw your own bad character, *astāghfirullāh*." It means, "Fix yourself." Then the *ḥadīth* came, *al-mu'min mirāta akhīhi*, "The *mu'min* is the mirror of his brother."

When you look at someone pious, your bad characteristics will appear. That is why when many people go to see Mawlana Shaykh Nazim ق they become frightened, because their memory is refreshed. How are you going to hide the bad things you have done in front of Mawlana Shaykh?

Awlīyāullāh take from that *ḥadīth* to polish the hearts of their *murīds*. They become a role model, a mirror reflecting the light of the one looking in it, and at the same time showing them their bad characteristics. That is why sitting with a guide shows you how many bad things you are doing, and it causes you to repent. When they look at you, you feel their presence and begin to remember all you did in the past and you begin to ask for forgiveness.

Sayyīdinā Abdul Qadir al-Jilani ق said, "What is this craziness, saying you don't need anyone to teach you?" Today they say, "Don't take a guide." Why not? The Prophet ﷺ took a guide when he moved from Mecca to Madinah; that was to teach us discipline. "I took a guide to Madinah, I took a guide to *qāba qawsayn*, I took Jibrīl ﷺ." Allāh ﷻ could have called the Prophet ﷺ without sending Jibrīl ﷺ, whom He sent for us to learn that we need a guide!

After reaching the Seven Heavens, Jibrīl ﷺ said, "I am not going any further," meaning, "There is no need for me anymore because you showed complete humbleness. I cannot go further because I will be burned." That is what we know, but in reality it means, "You don't need me anymore. You needed me so you could show your humbleness but you achieved that and now you don't need anyone; go wherever you like."

You say you don't need anyone to teach you, but the Prophet ﷺ said, "The *mu'min* is a mirror to his brother," which means you need that mirror to see where you are going. It is *sunnah* to look in the mirror and to thank Allāh ﷻ for giving you a very beautiful appearance. Allāh ﷻ gave everyone a very beautiful appearance, since no one can find a better one to suit himself or herself. Your appearance doesn't suit him, and his appearance doesn't suit another; each has an appearance unique to him and when that secret is opened that person becomes a spotlight, pulling people to Islam, to *maʿrifat*, out of darkness to the light. So you need each other.

You become a mirror when your faith reaches its peak and you have no doubt. All of us doubt many things, but the highest level of *imān* is to have no doubt in your heart!

Removing the Obstacle of Doubt

Sayyīdinā Imām al-Ghazālī's books are everywhere, even in areas where they don't accept *tasawwuf*. In the beginning of his life he was doubtful about everything: religion, Allāh's existence, even the Prophet ﷺ! Then he took a guide, Shaykh Yusūf al-Nassāj ق, his first teacher, who taught him, "Leave the *dunya* by your will before it leaves you by force (upon your death) and come to Sayyīdinā Muḥammad ﷺ."

Once at Ishrāq time, when the sun had risen, Prophet ﷺ took the Ṣaḥābah ؓ to Mt. Uhud and everyone had a shadow except the Prophet ﷺ. Then he told the Companions ؓ to face Mt. Uhud, and their shadows were in front of them. He said, "If anyone can catch his shadow, I will give him a reward. Run!" If someone said this to you, you would answer, "How can you catch your shadow? That is not possible." But they didn't ask, instead they said, *samiʿna wa ataʿna*, "We hear and we obey."

As they ran, they weren't able to catch their shadows until they reached the mountain, because the mountain was an obstacle and their shadows fell upon it and they caught them. Then the Prophet ﷺ said, "Turn and run towards me." They ran toward the Prophet ﷺ and their shadows ran after them. He said, "When you run after *dunya*, you can never catch your shadow as it runs from you, but when you run towards me your shadow, *dunya*, will run after you."

So we have to make sure we are not running after *dunya*, we must run towards the Prophet ﷺ! Then your heart will have the highest level of *imān* and at that time you will reflect whatever is in it and outside it for people to look at. You become a mirror for *khalāʾiq* people, and at the same time a mirror for yourself. That is a state of sainthood, but you must struggle for it.

Imām al-Ghazālī ؓ took the hand of his teacher, who said to him, "Leave *dunya* by your own choice, or else you will leave later by force." Imām al-Ghazālī returned home after ʿIsha and slept. He saw Allāh ﷻ in a dream, saying, "Yā Abū Ḥamīd! Leave *dunya* and come to Me." It was a long dream but this is the summary. He woke up very happy and he went to his *shaykh* to relate the dream to him. His *shaykh* said, "*Yā* Abū Ḥamīd, *hadhihi alwāhuna*, these are the Preserved Tablets which we observed and told you about. Because you were truthful in wanting to emerge from the state of doubtfulness, Allāh ﷻ sent you that dream. Before He sent you anything, this is what we were telling you about, 'Leave *dunya* before *dunya* leaves you by force.'"

From that moment all doubts dropped from his heart and he became one of the biggest *ʿālims* and one of the biggest Sufis. May Allāh ﷻ bless us to be always under their *maʿrifat*.

May Allāh ﷻ forgive us and may Allāh ﷻ bless us.

Wa min Allāhi ʿt-tawfiq, bi ḥurmati ʿl-ḥabīb, bi ḥurmati ʿl-Fātiḥah.

And with Allāh is success. For the sake of the Beloved, for his sake we recite the opening chapter of Holy Qur'an.

Divine Miracles and Mercy through the Awliya

Aʿūdhu billāhi min ash-Shayṭāni 'r-rajīm. Bismillāhi' r-Raḥmāni 'r-Raḥīm.
Nawaytu 'l-arbāʿīn, nawaytu 'l-ʿitikāf, nawaytu'l-khalwah, nawaytu 'l-ʿuzlah,
nawaytu 'r-riyāḍa, nawaytu 's-sulūk, lillāhi Taʿalā fī hādhā 'l-masjid.
Atīʿūllāha wa atīʿū 'r-Rasūla wa ūli 'l-amri minkum. (4:59)

The miraculous teachings in these pages were built on the sacrifice and devotion of past Naqshbandi saints who left their indelible signatures on Naqshbandi Ṭarīqah and the world.

Sayyidina `Abdul Khaliq al-Ghujdawani

Known throughout the world, Sayyīdinā ʿAbdul Khaliq al-Ghujdawani, may Allāh sanctify his soul, is the eleventh shaykh of the Naqshbandi Golden Chain. He is from Merv in Central Asia, a city on the way to Bukhara, Uzbekistan. There is a well at his *maqām* (tomb) famed for its healing powers, where even today hundreds visit to seek remedies for various illnesses. That well intentionally has only one cup from which to drink, and yet its visitors are not contaminated from others and many are cured.

Grandshaykh Sharafuddīn ق said there was an event on the night of *Laylat al-Raghayb*[3], the 7th of *Rajab*[4]. Muslims around the world honor that night, which occurred on Thursday (the night before Friday).

Sayyīdinā Shaykh Sharafuddīn ق narrated the following:

> That day the mother of Sayyīdinā ʿAbdul Khaliq al-Ghujdawani ق did laundry at the bank of the river. She took her son and looked after him very well as he played along the edge of the river. She saw an unknown man suddenly appear, speaking with her son, making him laugh and entertaining him, then suddenly both the man and her son both disappeared.

3 It is said in *Sīrat an-Nabī* (biography of Prophet Muhammad) that it is the night Prophet's Light passed from his father to his mother, Sayyida Amina ﵂ (to her womb; the blessed night of conception).

4 Seventh month of the Islamic calendar and one of the holiest.

She became frantic, searching along the riverbank for her son, but he was gone. She began to cry. At that moment, she saw a pious man coming towards her.

He said, "Why are you crying, O lady?"

She said, "My only child, my son, on account of whom I saw many miracles in my life, has now disappeared and I don't know what happened to him."

He said to her, "Why are you worried? Do you not know Allāh ﷻ takes care of pious people? Be patient, for if you are patient you will receive a lot of *khayr* (goodness). At the spiritual station you occupy, no one can become frustrated."

She asked, "Who are you?"

He said, "I am the prophet Ilyas."

She said, "May Allāh have mercy on you and us! Again, who are you?"

He replied, "Allāh prohibited the Earth to eat the flesh of prophets. We are alive, not dead. We can move about where we like."

She asked, "Can you tell me where is my son?"

He said, "Do you know what night this is?"

She answered, "No."

He said, "This is the night of the sixth of *Rajab*, in which good desires are fulfilled. On that night, Allāh ﷻ sends on the *ummāh* such mercy that the angels of the Seven Heavens are carrying blessings on human beings so great that no one can count them other than Allāh ﷻ!

"On that night the *nutfat an-Nabī* (pure atom of the Prophet ﷺ) passed from his father to his mother's womb. On that night, Allāh orders all angels, all prophets and all *awlīyā* to meet in *Kaʿabatullāh* to receive the Prophet's ﷺ *barakah* (blessing). Although he is still young, your son is one of the great *awlīyā* of his time. Khidr[5], whom you saw speaking to your son, carried him to Mecca. He was transferred from Merv to Mecca in the blink of an eye! There he is going to see all these prophets, angels and *awlīyā*, and will inherit his share of sainthood from him. Be happy!"

She asked, "When will he come back?"

5 One of the holiest, most knowledgeable saints in Islam who learned directly from God.

He said, "After *sahūr*[6] he will return."[7]

She left and went home.

Sayyīdinā ʿAbdul Khaliq al-Ghujdawani ق was carried by Sayyīdinā Khidr ﷺ and given in turn from one *walī* to another, and afterwards from one prophet to another, until he reached the presence of Sayyīdinā Muhammad ﷺ. Each *walī* enhanced his spiritual level and his heart's lights, until he was prepared to meet the Prophet ﷺ.

Sayyīdinā ʿAbdul Khaliq al-Ghujdawani ق was a descendant of the *Ṣahābi*, Malik bin Sinan al-Ansari ﷺ. The Prophet ﷺ hugged him in his arms and ordered all the spirits of the *Ṣahābah* to come forth. As soon as they appeared, he was carried from one to another, until he reached the hands of Malik bin Sinan al-Ansari, who carried him to Rasūlullāh[8] ﷺ, who said, "We are very happy and honored that this son is from our descendants."

Then ʿAbdul Khaliq ق went from one hand to another, until daylight appeared, and by means of the spiritual power of conveyance of Sayyīdinā Khidr, he was returned to his home.

His mother saw him and said, "O my son! I asked Prophet Ilyas ﷺ to give me a blessing and he said to me, 'On that night there are many groups of angels and no one knows their number except Allāh, and they are constantly busy in worship in every moment. They commit no sins and they are each in different aspects of *ṣalāt*. Some are in *rukuʿ*, some are in *qiyam*, some are in *sajda*, some are in *jalsa*, and some are making *tashahhud* (attestation of God's Unity).

'For the sake of your son, Allāh is going to share the worship of all these angels, and it will be written on your shoulders. Allāh the Exalted will grant a share of the *tasbīḥ* (glorification) of the angels up to the Judgment Day to anyone who follows the way of your son (Naqshbandi Way).'"

Sayyīdinā ʿAbdul Khaliq, who was quite young, replied, "Mother, what Allāh opened to me from the *barakah* of the Prophet ﷺ is a drop of an ocean."

---

6 The meal before sunrise, in preparation for the fast.

7 Customarily, many Muslims fast that following day.

8 Lit. "Messenger of Allah;" a popular reference to Prophet Muhammad ﷺ.

Shaykh Sharafuddīn ق said *Laylat al-Bara'ah*[9], the Night of Innocence, is mentioned in the Qur'an:

In that (Night) is decreed every affair of wisdom. (Sūrat ad-Dukhān, 44:4)

In that night, Allāh informs the angels of what will take place in the coming year. It is the 14th of *Sha'bān*[10]. The first to show its purpose, after the *Ṣahābah* and the *Tabi'īn* was Imām Isma'il al-Bukhari, the pre-imminent *imām* of *hadith.* Here, Shaykh Sharafuddīn ق is narrating from what Sayyīdinā Imām Isma'il al-Bukhāri said, passing from the heart of one *walī* to another, until it reached the heart of Shaykh Sharafuddīn ق more than 1200 years later.

The Happy Angels and Power of Abi Zamzam

Shaykh Sharafuddīn ق said, "On that holy night Allāh created a group of angels known as *al-Malā'ikatis-Suayyda,* the Happy Angels. They were created exclusively to serve Sayyīdinā Muhammad ﷺ. Their sole assignment was to inspire Sayyida Amina ؓ to seek a nursemaid for her newborn son, and to arrange for Sayyida Halima as-Sa'adiyya to suckle the Prophet ﷺ.

This is proof *Allāhu ar-razzaq dhul quwwatta al-matīn,* Allāh is the Provider of great strength. Allāh ﷻ created angels specifically to provide sustenance for the Prophet ﷺ in his childhood, and to inspire his grandfather, 'Abdul Muttalib ؓ, and his uncle, Abū Talib ؓ, to be his great supporters. The Happy Angels were also granted authority by Allāh ﷻ to make the heavenly powers of *al-Kawthar*[11] flow from Halima as-Sa'adiyya ؓ to Sayyīdinā Muhammad ﷺ, and from *al-Kawthar* to the well of *Zamzam*[12]. Hence, *Abi Zamzam* is rejuvenated every 14th *Sha'bān* by means of those angels.

In the time before the Prophet ﷺ, that night was known as "*Laylat al-Birr,*" Night of the Well. After the Prophet's ﷺ birth it became known as

9 Also known in some countries as "*Shab-i-Bara'at*"; '*shab*' is Persian for "night."

10 The Islamic month which precedes Ramaḍān .

11 A river in Paradise which has honey-like milk.

12 "*Abi Zamzam:*" a free-flowing well that appeared in Mecca for Isma'il, son of Abraham, known for its miraculous healing powers.

"Laylat al-Bara'ah", Night of Innocence, as it is the night on which the well of *Zamzam* fills up.

Ka'b al-Ahbar ❁ relates, "Allāh ❁ created the well of *Zamzam* for Sayyīdinā Muhammad ❁, specifically to bring the holy water of *Kawthar* there. In his infancy, when Sayyīdinā Isma'il was left in the desert of Mecca with no provision, by Allāh's command he kicked the sand with the heel of his tiny foot, causing the well of *Zamzam* to gush forth. Anyone who drinks its miraculous water will go to Paradise."

In recent times when the well of *Zamzam* was explored by scientists, they found the water gushing forth inside its narrow cavity like high-pressure jets and they could not locate the source.

Laylat al-Bara'ah is also known as the "Night of Freedom," because on that night Allāh sets sinners free from the fire of Hell and from hypocrisy, and sends them to Paradise. That great blessing of salvation is due to the source of *Zamzam* being from the Heavenly River, *al-Kawthar*. That unique, blessed milk is composed nine-tenths from the water of *al-Kawthar*, brought by the Happy Angels to the breast of Sayyida Halima as-Sa'adiyya ❁, and one-tenth normal breast milk. Because of that, the Prophet ❁ grew in one month as much as most children grow in nine months.

Secrets of Laylat al-Bara'ah

One of the most important occasions in the Islamic calendar, *Laylat al-Bara'ah*, occurs on 15 *Sha'bān*[13]. About its significance, Shaykh Sharafuddīn ق said that Allāh ❁ makes known the sustenance for all human beings and all living species, which then appears on *al-Lawh al-Mahfūẓ*, the Preserved Tablets[14]. Even if an ant is going to break its leg, it is written on the Preserved Tablets, specifying the location, the country, the exact detail where and when that ant will break its leg, and everything must be arranged for that event by angels.

In that night all the doors are opened and the water of the heavenly river *al-Kawthar* flows down to Earth and floods the well of *Zamzam*. In that

13 The eighth month of the Islamic calendar, which follows Rajab and precedes Ramaḍān.

14 The Divine Tablets upon which everything is recorded from the beginning to the end of time.

night the names of "happy ones," those who will be saved[15], will appear on the Preserved Tablets, meaning they will be raised to the level of *awliyā*[16].

Shaykh Sharafuddīn ق said:

Sayyīdinā Abū Bakr as-Ṣiddīq [17] ؓ asked Kaʿb al-Ahbar ؓ, the trusted scribe of the Divine Revelations[18], "O Kaʿb al-Ahbar! Do you know the numbers of the Happy Angels?"

Prophet ﷺ replied, "O Abū Bakr! Their leaders, not counting their followers, are created by Allāh on the number of stars He created from the beginning of Creation until Judgment Day, as many as He created and is creating. So then calculate how many their followers are! All of them are praising Allāh and praying on the Prophet, and all of the rewards for that are written for the *Ummāh*[19] of Muhammad ﷺ."

Those leaders, as many as all created stars, along with their followers, were bringing the water of *al-Kawthar* from Paradise, with all its knowledge and light, and channeling it to the breasts of Sayyida Halima as-Saʿadiyya ؓ. From that source, Prophet ﷺ knew all the *ʿUlum al-Awwalīn wa ʾl-Ākhirīn*, Knowledge of the Firsts and Lasts (Beginning to the End; all matters)[20].

The following came through spiritual inspirations and visions to Shaykh Sharafuddīn ق, who beheld Kaʿb al-Ahbar ؓ saying:

Allāh ﷻ was sending the vision of beauty, power and majesty. The Ninety-Nine Beautiful Names and Attributes[21] were sent to the *Nahr al-Kawthar*[22] raising up its level with its *tajallīyat*[23] and blessings, sending those

---

15 *as-sūʿada*, "the saved."

16 Saints; lit. "friends of God."

17 The first man to embrace Islam; Prophet Muhammad's closest friend and father-in-law; Naqshbandi Ṭarīqah flows through him.

18 *al-wāhi*, the Divine Revelation that descended to the Prophet ﷺ, and which ceased after he departed from this world.

19 The nation of Muhammad ﷺ. Sent as a "Mercy to All the Worlds," his nation includes all humanity.

20 Narrated by Ibn ʿUmar by Ahmad, at-Tabarani in the *Kabir* (12:361), Haythami in *Majmaʿ al-Zawaʾid*, Ibn Kathir in his *Tafsir*, and Suyuti in his *Tafsir al-Durr al-Manthur*, that the Prophet ﷺ said, "I have received the keys to everything (unseen) except the Five (which Allah alone knows)." Haythami said, "The sub-narrators in Ahmad's chain are the men of sound narration."

21 Divine Manifestations of Allah to His Creation, as He wishes to be known.

22 The honey-like milk that flows in the River Kawthar in Paradise.

23 Heavenly emanations from the Divine Presence.

blessings to the water of *al-Kawthar* in Paradise 366 times. The entire purpose of that was, in the future, when Prophet ﷺ drank that water from the breast of Halima as-Saʿadiyya, he received the power to control the hardest hearts of human beings. That is why he ﷺ was sent to the people possessing the hardest hearts on Earth, *ahli Makkah*[24], the Bedouins, in order to soften their hearts. That is why for so many years they tortured the Prophet ﷺ and his Companions ؓ.

Those Happy Angels and their uncounted number known solely to Allāh ﷻ will come to *Masjid al-Aqsa*[25] and pray in that mosque, and mention by name every single member of the *ummah* of Prophet ﷺ, and seek Allāh's forgiveness for them. Then they will go to the roof of *Kaʿaba* with Sayyīdinā Jibrīl[26] ؑ, and ask Allāh in a special *duʿa* to forgive *Ummat an-Nabī* ﷺ. This they have repeated every year from the time of the Prophet ﷺ and they will continue up to Judgment Day.

After visiting *Masjid al-Aqsa* and the *Kaʿaba*, then they travel to *Madinat al-Munawwara*[27] to the *Rawdat ash-Sharifah*, the Prophet's ﷺ holy grave[28], and wait for him to emerge. Then he ﷺ emerges from the dome of the grave with his four caliphs and 124,000 *Ṣahābah*. There, in front of that vast procession of angels, Prophet ﷺ will mention the name of each member of his nation, saying, "*Yā Rabbil ʿizzati wal-ʿadhamati wal jabarūt*, forgive them." He will ask Allāh to give his nation two virtues: innocence from Hellfire and innocence from hypocrisy.

Then Allāh ﷻ will reply, "I have freed your *ummah* from Hellfire and I have freed them from hypocrisy." That is in their spiritual life, not their physical life, as they have the ego controlling them and for this reason aspects of hypocrisy still appear from their egoistic selves.

Then Allāh ﷻ will make these angels and Companions visit each and every person alive or dead, in their home or in their grave, and whatever worship these angels are doing will be granted to each member of *Ummat an-Nabī* ﷺ.

---

24 The people of Mecca (who lived there at that time).

25 Holy sanctuary in Jerusalem, to where the Prophet ﷺ miraculously traveled from Madinah, and from where he performed the Holy Ascension, *Miʾrāj*. The third holiest place in Islam.

26 Archangel Gabriel.

27 The holy city Madinah, known as "the Prophet's city" and "City of Light"; the second holiest site in Islam after Mecca.

28 One of the holiest sites in Islam, believed part of Heaven.

Then Prophet ﷺ will request, "O Allāh! Give the reward of the water of *Zamzam* to all the members of my *ummāh*." Allāh will say, "*Yā Habibi*. I gave you an *ummāh* that makes sins, and they repent and I forgive them. I am going to make from every drop of *Zamzam* powers to waive all sins: even if you drink one drop of the water of *Zamzam*, it has the power to clean you of all sins you make in all your life (as it is mixed with the water of *al-Kawthar*)." *(This concludes the testimony of Kaʿb al-Ahbar.)*

One drop of *Zamzam* is heavier in the Divine Scale than the mountain of Uhud[29]. For that reason, it is very important to remain awake throughout the night of *Laylat Baraʿah*, to pray one hundred *rakaʿats* of specified prayers and to fast its day. If one cannot achieve this, he may sleep and recite, "O my Lord, I am a weak servant and cannot do what should be done," and Allāh will forgive him.

One of the great *awlīyā*, Maʿruf al-Karkhi ق, said, "Whoever stays up all of the night of *Laylat al-Baraʿah* and fasts its day, Allāh will give them the reward of someone struggling *fī sabīlillāh*[30] for forty years."

It is said another great *walī*, Ibrahim al-Khawwas ق, was calling on Allāh fervently in his *munājāt*[31], saying, "Show me Imām al-Ghazali. Let me see Imām Abū Hamid al-Ghazali!" Al-Khawwas beheld Imām Ghazali in a vision and asked, "O *imām*, what is the most superior deed in addition to the five obligations?" Imām Ghazali replied:

> *Inna Allāha wa malāʿikatahu yuṣallūna ʿalá an-nabīyyi yā ʿayyuhā al-ladhīna ʿāmanū ṣallū ʿalayhi wa sallimū taslīmā.*
>
> *Allāh sends His Ṣalāt (graces, honors, blessings, mercy, etc.) on the Prophet (Muhammad) as do His angels (ask Allāh to bless and forgive him). O you who believe! Send your Ṣalāt on him (ask Allāh to bless Muhammad), and salute him with all respect (saying, as-salāmuʿalaykum!).*
>
> (Sūrat al-Ahzāb, 33:56)

That verse was revealed in the month *Shaʿbān*. Anyone who recites it and praises the Prophet ﷺ, Allāh will praise him ten times and mention him

29 A mountain located on the outskirts of Madinah, where a significant battle was waged in the early years of Islam in which some Companions of the Prophet were martyred.

30 In the Way of Allah, the highest level of action.

31 Invocation in verse.

ten times, and make his heart *madhharan litajallī ar-raḥmān*[32], full of the blessings and manifestations of Allāh's Name *"ar-Raḥmān."*[33] Whatever manifestation is on the Throne of *ar-Raḥmān* will be manifested to the servant who obeys that order, *'sallu alayhi was sallimu taslīmah.'*

During *Laylat al-Bara'ah,* Prophet ﷺ calls upon his *ummāh,* mentioning each of its members one-by-one, and he asks Allāh to forgive them. And he asks to come nearer to the Divine Presence and Allāh grants permission to come to the right side of *'Arsh ar-Raḥmān, kāna Qāba Qawsayni aw Adna.* There, Prophet ﷺ will call for a grand assembly of the inhabitants of *Barzākh*[34] whose souls are free due to their excessive worship, and they will reach that *tajallī* without seeing it. From *dunyā*[35] no one will be able to attend that assembly except seven *awlīyā* from the 124,000 saints who live in every century, to whom Allāh will grant entry. These *awlīyā* will witness the proceedings in order to reveal it to their followers, and one of them was our grandshaykh, Sayyīdinā Shaykh Sharafuddīn ق.

The prayers of Prophet ﷺ on that night are *fi haqq jam'i al-ummam*[36], from the time of Adam عليه السلام up to the Day of Judgment. Whoever the Prophet ﷺ mentions by name will be of the highest level of people on the Day of Gathering, and they are of one-hundred different kinds, each of them under one of the manifestations of the Ninety-Names of Allāh, and Prophet ﷺ will be under the manifestation of *Isma 'l-'Ādham,* the Greatest Name, "Allāh."

As per the Qur'an, on that night Allāh will order the moon to make *tasbīh*[37]:

> *The Seven Heavens and the Earth and all therein praise Him, and there is not a thing but sings his praise, but you understand not their praise. Lo! He is Ever-Clement, Forgiving.* (Sūrat al-Isrā', 17:44)

Every stone of the moon will make *tasbīḥ* and will be ordered to make *istāghfār*[38] for every member of the *ummāh,* which is more valuable than the *istāghfār* of forty *siddiqs*[39]!

---

32 An image of the manifestation of *al-Rahman*.

33 "The Most Compassionate," one of God's principle attributes through which He wants to be known.

34 Where souls remain after leaving the physical world, awaiting Judgment Day.

35 The physical world.

36 For the sake of all nations.

37 Supplication; praise.

38 Seeking forgiveness.

If those seven *awlīyā* mention the name of a person on the Day of Judgment, he or she will be among the *Amānat al-Ummāh*[40], able to bring many people under the *shafaʿa* of Prophet ﷺ For their sake, Allāh will forgive many people on the Day of Judgment.

Yusuf al-Hamadani, who was one of the *awlīyā* attending that gathering, narrated:

> For twenty-four years, I attended that grand assembly on the right hand of the Throne, but I had a question: I did not know what river was flowing on the right side of the Throne.
>
> One of the seven *awlīyā* who attends that assembly, Bayazid al-Bistami[41] answered, "That is the river of Shaʿbān."
>
> I asked, "How long is that river?"
>
> Bayazid al-Bistami ق answered, "It is 7,000 years in length. I used to pray two *rakaʿats* there every night with the *awlīyā* and the prophets who bring them. After the two *rakaʿats,* we found the water of that river decreasing. Why? Because Allāh orders all the angels of Paradise to take a shower in that river of Shaʿbān, according to the *hadith,* "*Shaʿbānu shahri*[42]." Whoever washes in that river is under the authority of the Prophet ﷺ and will be granted forgiveness."

May Allāh forgive us and make us understand the words of the *awlīyā*! Some ignorant people say the intercession of Prophet ﷺ is only applied on Judgment Day, but we say it is relevant every moment!

In the (Night) is made distinct every affair of wisdom.

(Sūrat ad-Dukhān, 44:4)

This verse is a reference to Allāh's placing on *Laylat al-Baraʿah* everything that will happen during that year on the Preserved Tablets, and everyone will be granted intercession by Prophet ﷺ and takes a share of the mercy which he is sending to the *ummāh.*

---

39 Pious people.

40 Trust of the Nation of Prophet ﷺ.

41 Sixth shaykh in the Naqshbandi Golden Chain.

42 The saying of the Prophet ﷺ, "Sha'ban is my month."

The sacred *Laylat al-Qadr*, "the Night of Power" occurs once each year in the last ten days of the holy month, Ramaḍān. To any Naqshbandi *murīd* who spends that night in worship, Allāh grants the equivalent of worship of the 124,000 living *awlīyā* with all the combined worship of their entire lives!

Sayyidina Shah Naqshband

Sayyīdinā Shah Naqshband ق, *imām* of the Naqshbandi Sufi Order, is a rare scholar of *'Ilm ash-Shari'ah*[43] and *'Ilm al-Haqīqah*[44]. He was known as *Dhu-Janahayn*, "Possessor of Two Wings," keeping two sorts of knowledge: one he shares with all and one he keeps for his followers. He was also known as *Sultān al-'Arifīn*, King of the Gnostics.

Sayyīdinā Shaykh Sharafuddīn ق relates the *hadith*:

Whenever the awlīyā are mentioned, the mercy of Allāh descends on that group.[45]

That is because they are mentioning His saints. Where that mercy descends is one of the secrets revealed by Sayyīdinā Grandshaykh Sharafuddīn ق and Grandshaykh 'AbdAllāh al-Fa'iz ad-Daghestani ق during their seclusions, when they received secrets from their shaykhs and from Prophet ﷺ.

Grandshaykh Sharafuddīn ق said, "When the stories of the saints and details of their lives are mentioned, the sins of the listeners will be shattered away like the shattering of glass."

Being a great scholar in his time, he mentioned that Ibn Hajar al-Haytami often traveled one or two days (then they measured distance in time or days), to hear the stories narrated by Naqshbandi shaykhs. One such story is regarding Muhammad Bahauddin an-Naqshband (Shah Naqshband) of Bukhara, presently Uzbekistan.

When he reached the age of seven years, Shah Naqshband was brought to meet with all the spirits of *anbīyaullāh*[46] and messengers in the presence of Sayyīdinā Muhammad ﷺ, where age is not significant, only the spirit is significant. Thus, Shah Naqshband arrived in that Holy Presence at age

43 The Science of Islamic Divine Law.

44 The Science of Divine Reality.

45 Ibn Khuzaymah in the introduction to his *Safwat as-Safa*.

46 God's prophets.

seven: he was unique, for no one could match his level among all Naqshbandis of that time.⁴⁷

There in the presence of the Prophet ﷺ, Sayyīdinā Musa ؑ⁴⁸ asked Shah Naqshband, "*Yā fard al-'alam*! When were you chosen as a guide for humanity?"⁴⁹

Shah Naqshband replied, "I was a *murshid*⁵⁰ when *awlīyā* were in complete non-existence," meaning, "I was *murshid* before Allāh created the *awlīyā*." He was not speaking about himself, but rather of the secret of the Prophet ﷺ that was passed to him at that level, in that unique state of ecstasy.

Then Sayyīdinā Musa said, "Explain; we want to know."

Sayyīdinā Shah Naqshband ق descends from the line of Sayyīdinā Abū Bakr as-Ṣiddīq ق, so out of *adab*⁵¹ for Sayyīdinā Musa, Abū Bakr answered, "O Musa! When Shah Naqshband spoke to you, it was from the level he inherited from Prophet ﷺ ⁵² and from that level is one of forty-six parts of *nubuwwat*.⁵³ From the secret of that level, he answered you." Then Abū Bakr ق looked at Sayyīdinā Shah Naqshband, indicating permission to respond to the questions.

Shah Naqshband ق replied, "I was a *murshid*⁵⁴ when there were no *awlīyā*, before granting the *awlīyā* their position in *Yawma Alastu bi Rabbikum*, the Day of Promises⁵⁵. Even then Allāh allowed me to look after my followers and their sustenance, and guide them when the *awlīyā* were yet in void."

Sayyīdinā Musa repeated, "Explain."

---

47 For that reason, among *awlīyāullāh* he is titled "*Farḍ al-'Alam*," meaning, "unique among Creation" or, "*Farḍ al-'Arsh*," meaning, "unique one at the Divine Throne."

48 Prophet Moses, upon whom be peace.

49 This means "teacher" or "guide," not a prophet or messenger. *Saḥābah* are the highest rank after prophets, then saints.

50 One who bestows *irshād* (guidance); a spiritual guide.

51 Etiquette; protocol.

52 Referring to the famous *hadith* of Prophet Muhammad, "Never was anything revealed to me that I did not pour into the heart of Abu Bakr."

53 The Prophet ﷺ said that a true dream is one of forty-six parts of prophethood.

54 Spiritual guide, a shaykh.

55 When every soul stood before God and pledged eternal faith in His Unity, before being sent into this world, as mentioned in Holy Qur'an 7:172.

Sayyīdinā Naqshband ق continued, "I was given my station of sainthood before every *walī* was given his station of sainthood from the Naqshbandi Order. And I received that when I was still in the World of Atoms[56]. Allāh created me before He had yet created the Naqshbandi *awlīyā* by 20,000 years and I was under the *tarbīyyah* and *ināyat* of Prophet ﷺ. Allāh then created all other *awlīyā* and they appeared after 17,000 years. There is a difference of 10,000 years between my reality's appearance and theirs. That is what I meant."

That occurred when Shah Naqshband ق was seven years old, and it was his first *irshād*[57] in the presence of *anbīya,* the *awliyāullāh* and *Ṣahābah.*

Allāh ﷻ granted Shah Naqshband 12,000 specialties. One of the most basic specialties, in order to give you an idea of the others, is the power to focus his vision around the universe 363 times every 24 hours, to observe all Creation. He observes what they are doing, the state of their sustenance, their affairs, their problems and difficulties, and to look after every baby in the womb of its mother.

On that occasion of his first visit, Shah Naqshband ق asked, "O my Lord, don't let anyone who takes me as a guide and those who came after me or before me exist without support from You." All the angels of the skies said, "*Amīn.*"

Grandshaykh, may Allāh sanctify his soul, said the *barakah* and protection of that *du'a* appears four times a year to the followers of Shah Naqshband: on 14 Muharram (Shah Naqshband's birthday); on the first day of Ramaḍān, on 15 Ramaḍān and on *Laylat al-Qadr.* Whoever entered the Naqshbandi Ṭarīqah will be protected from all sides!

When Allāh ﷻ created the *awlīyā,* after 17,000 years (10,000 years after Shah Naqshband's creation), they came to the World of Essence, spoke to the essence of Shah Naqshband and asked him for the sake of Sayyīdinā Muhammad ﷺ to be accepted in the Naqshbandi Ṭarīqah. He accepted 7,007 of them to be saints, whereupon each of them was granted 12,000 knowledge's from every letter of Qur'an they read.

Shah Naqshband ق sought this distinction for the sake of Prophet ﷺ, and when he requested this, Prophet ﷺ looked at him and raised him for

---

56 *'alam adh-dhārr,* when people were in the essence of their realities.

57 His first association; *suḥbat.*

every letter of Qur'an multiplied by the 12,000 knowledge's given on each letter to these *awlīyā!*

We say there are 70,000 veils of darkness between us and the presence of Prophet ﷺ. As much as you become nearer to him, the last veil makes you feel you are very far from his reality, for to be near to the presence of Prophet ﷺ, your *ishq*[58] will make you feel even farther away from him.

From that station of knowledge Shah Naqshband revealed, "When *awliyāullāh* destroy those veils and approach the presence of Prophet ﷺ, there are 700,000 more veils to overcome to reach the essence of the presence of Prophet ﷺ. I crossed where no one reached before."

Sayyīdinā Bayazid al-Bistami

When Sayyīdinā Bayazid ق was stoned and tortured by his tribe, he boarded a ship and prayed, "O My Lord! Take me to a place where I will feel happy." Thereafter, the ship began to toss about on the high waves. The ship's captain said, "There must be a great sinner on board who is causing this calamity!"

Sayyīdinā Bayazid al-Bistami ق said, "I am that sinner; throw me in the ocean."

He said to himself, "I am going into that ocean and will seek the Presence of Allāh." As soon as he was thrown in, the water stopped tossing about, and without thinking of any other purpose and using his utmost spiritual power, Sayyīdinā Bayazid began to plunge into that ocean faster than the speed of light, until he reached a place of ultimate darkness and void. There he heard a voice which Grandshaykh ق described as, "*Huuuuuuuuuuuuuuuuuu.*"

Sayyīdinā Bayazid ق was granted extraordinary spiritual powers, similar to those of Shah Naqshband ق, powers which he tried to use to count the number of all the people at that location saying "*Huuuu.*" Despite using all his power, he could not count them. Grandshaykh ق says Sayyīdinā Bayazid ق then realized this was a presence he could not reach and he knew it was Shah Naqshband ق and his followers reciting "*Huuuu.*"

Although Shah Naqshband came many centuries after Sayyīdinā Bayazid al-Bistami ق, still he reached Shah Naqshband's spiritual presence

58 Love in the purest form.

and that of his *murīds*. Sayyīdinā Bayazid al-Bistami ق was worried, anticipating Shah Naqshband ق would ask him why he was there and send him away, for *awlīyā* guard their followers fiercely and don't want another *walī* in their territory.

Sayyidina Qasim bin Muhammad bin Abu Bakr

Sayyīdinā Qasim bin Muhammad bin Abū Bakr as-Ṣiddīq ق follows Salmān al-Farsi ق in the Naqshbandi Golden Chain. His paternal grandfather is Abū Bakr as-Ṣiddīq ق and his maternal grandfather is Sayyīdinā ʿAlī bin Talib ق. He was born on a Thursday in Ramaḍān, 38 Hijri, and left this world on Thursday, 9 Muharram, 108 Hijri.

It is narrated by our Grandshaykhs:

Sayyīdinā Qasim ق said, "My grandfather, Abū Bakr as-Ṣiddīq ق, had been all alone with Prophet ﷺ. Once when he was in Ghari Thawr[59] during migration, Prophet said to him, "You have been with me all your life and in all your difficulties. I now want you to recite a *duʿa,* for which Allāh will bestow a favor upon you and your descendants."

Abū Bakr then said, "*Yā Rasūlullāh* (O Messenger of God)! You are the secret of my soul and of my heart. You know better what I need."

Prophet ﷺ raised his hands and said, "*Yā* Allāh (O God!), as long as my Shariʿah proceeds to Judgment Day[60], may Allāh grant from your descendants those who carry the Shariʿah and those who inherit its inner side, and grant from your descendants those who are on the *Sirāt al-Mustaqīm*[61] and those who guide to it."

The first to answer that *duʿa* and become that descendant was Sayyīdinā Qasim ق. In his time, he was known in Madinah as "Abū Muhammad." There was no one comparable to him in knowledge; he was among seven of the highest in knowledge, including Zaid bin Qasim, and Sulayman bin Yassar, Sayyīdinā Qasim being the highest.

People came to listen to his guidance, his *suḥbat* and his revelations of the hidden meanings of the Qur'an.

---

59 A cave between Mecca and Madinah where the Prophet and Abū Bakr hid safely during their migration, with members of the Quraysh tribe in hot pursuit, intending to kill them.

60 God said, *inna nahnu nazalna al-dhirk wa inna lahu lahāfidhūn,* the Divine Law is protected up to Judgment Day.

61 The Straight Path to God.

In this manuscript from which we are narrating, Grandshaykh Sharafuddīn and Grandshaykh ʿAbdAllāh ad-Daghestani ق tell the following story.

The year in which Abū Muhammad Qasim ق was to leave *dunyā*, on the third of Ramaḍān he departed for Hajj. When he thereafter arrived at *al-Qudayd*[62], Allāh opened to his sight angels coming down from Heaven and going up in numbers that no one can describe. They come down, visit the place and go up. As Abū Muhammad Qasim ق beheld those angels with all the blessings Allāh was sending down with them, it was as if the light and their power was so concentrated and it poured into his heart directly, filling it with *yaqīn* and *taqwa*[63].

As soon as this occurred, he fell asleep. He saw in a dream Sayyīdinā Abū Bakr as-Ṣiddīq ق, his grandfather, coming to him. He said, "O my Grandfather, who are these heavenly beings coming down and going up, filling my heart with *taqwa*?"

Abū Bakr as-Ṣiddīq ق answered, "Those angels you see ascending and descending Allāh assigned to be the constant visitors at your grave. They are getting *barakah* from where your body is going to be buried in the Earth. As *tadhīm*[64] for you, Allāh ordered them to come down and seek blessings for you. O my grandson, don't be heedless about your death! It is coming soon and you are going to be raised to the Divine Presence and leave *dunyā*."

Sayyīdinā Qasim ق immediately opened his eyes and saw his grandfather in front of him. He said, "I just saw you in the dream."

Sayyīdinā Abū Bakr as-Ṣiddīq ق replied, "Yes, I was ordered to meet you."

"That means I am going to leave this *dunyā*," answered Sayyīdinā Qasim ق.

"Yes, you are going to leave *dunyā* and accompany us to the Hereafter," replied Sayyīdinā Abū Bakr as-Ṣiddīq ق.

"What kind of *ʿāmal* do you advise I should perform in the last moments I am on Earth?" asked Sayyīdinā Qasim ق.

62 A common rest stop for pilgrims traveling to Mecca.

63 Sincerity and piety.

64 Great honor.

Sayyīdinā Abū Bakr as-Ṣiddīq ق answered, "O my son, keep your tongue moistened with *dhikrullāh* and keep your heart ready and present with *dhikrullāh*! That is the best you can ever achieve in this *dunyā*."

Then Sayyīdinā Abū Bakr ق disappeared and Sayyīdinā Qasim ق began *dhikr* on his tongue and in his heart. He continued to Mecca and witnessed ʿArafat[65]. That year many *awlīyā* were spiritually present at ʿArafat, both men and women saints, and Sayyīdinā Qasim ق met with them. As they were all standing at ʿArafat, suddenly all who were present heard distinct crying, a very plaintive bellow. Every saint who was present heard it clearly, and some asked the plain of ʿArafat (*Sahl ʿArafat*), "Why are you crying in this strange way?"

Sahl ʿArafat replied, "We and all angels are crying, because today this Earth is going to lose one of its pillars."

They asked, "Who is that pillar the Earth will lose?"

Sahl ʿArafat replied, "Abū Muhammad Qasim is going to leave this *dunyā* and it will no longer be honored with his steps, and I will no longer see him on my plain to where all pilgrims come, and I will miss him. That is why I am crying in this way! He inherits from his grandfather Sayyīdinā Muhammad ﷺ and his grandfather Abū Bakr and his grandfather Sayyīdinā ʿAlī, and the whole world is crying! They say the death of a scholar is the death of the world."

At that moment the spiritual presence of Prophet ﷺ and of Abū Bakr as-Ṣiddīq ق were present on ʿArafat, crying. Prophet ﷺ said, "With the death of Qasim, there will appear too much corruption throughout Earth. He was one of the pillars able to prevent corruption."

May Allāh forgive us and grant us the *barakah* of Sayyīdinā Qasim bin Muhammad bin Abū Bakr as-Ṣiddīq! *Bi hurmatil Fātiḥah.*

That crying of *Sahl ʿArafat* only occurred when Prophet ﷺ passed from this *dunyā*, then when Sayyīdinā Abū Bakr passed, then when Sayyīdinā Salmān passed, and when Sayyīdinā Qasim passed!

One of the *awlīyā*, Rabiʿa al-Adawiyya ق, asked to meet with Sayyīdinā Qasim ق in the spiritual assembly of *awlīyā*. Sayyīdinā Qasim said, "I heard every dry thing and living thing crying. Why, O Rabiʿa, did this happen? I never experienced such crying in my life! Do you know why we are hearing such crying?"

---

65 Mount Arafat outside of Mecca, a holy site where pilgrims atone as an integral rite of pilgrimage.

She replied, "O Abū Muhammad! I also was not able to comprehend that crying. You must ask your grandfather, Sayyīdinā Abū Bakr."

Sayyīdinā Abū Bakr appeared spiritually, saying, "That crying from every point on this Earth is because you are leaving this *dunyā*, as I informed you on your pilgrimage."

Then Sayyīdinā Qasim raised his hands and prayed to Allāh ﷻ, "Since I am passing away from this life now, forgive whoever stood with me on *Sahl ʿArafat.*"

Then they heard a voice saying, "For your sake, Allāh has forgiven whoever stood with you on *Sahl ʿArafat* on this Hajj." At that moment, Allāh revealed to Sayyīdinā Qasim's heart *al-mawahib*[66], dressing him. Then he departed from *Sahl ʿArafat*, saying, "O Mount ʿArafat, don't forget me on Judgment Day! All *awlīyā* and *anbīya* stood here, and so I ask you not to forget me on Judgment Day."

That huge mountain in that vast valley replied in a loud voice that everyone could hear, "*Yā* Qasim! Don't forget me on the Judgment Day, don't forget me, let me be part of the *shafaʿa*[67] of Sayyīdinā Muhammad ﷺ!"

At that moment, Sayyīdinā Qasim departed to the *Kaʿaba* in Mecca al-Mukarrama. There, he heard crying coming from the House of Allāh, which increased in loudness more and more as he approached. Everyone heard it. That was the voice of the *Kaʿaba,* crying for his passing, and its tears began to pour forth, flooding the entire area with water.

It said, "O Qasim! I am going to miss you and I am not going to see you again in this *dunyā*."

Then the *Kaʿaba* made 500 *tawāf*[68] around Sayyīdinā Qasim out of respect for him. *Kaʿabatullāh* respects *awlīyā* because it is living and can be heard. Whenever a *walī* visits *Kaʿaba* it responds to that *walī's salām*[69], saying *wa alayka as-salām ya walī-ūllāh,* "And Peace be with you, O Friend of Allāh."

Then Sayyīdinā Qasim ق said farewell to the *Hajar al-Aswad*[70] and to *Jannat al-Muʿalla* where Sayyida Khadijah al-Kubra ﵂[71] is buried. Then he

66 Gnostic knowledge, without count.

67 Intercession.

68 Ritual counter-clockwise circumambulation of Kaʿaba as performed in the pilgrimage.

69 The greeting *as-salamu alaykum*, "Peace be with you."

70 The Black Stone from Heaven, originally laid in place by Prophet Abraham and his son, Ishma'il ﵉.

71 Prophet Muhammad's first wife and mother of his children.

said farewell to all of Mecca. Then he left and went to *al-Qudayd* on 9th Muharram, a Thursday.

May Allāh ﷻ forgive us and may Allāh ﷻ bless us.

Wa min Allāhi 't-tawfīq, bi ḥurmati 'l-ḥabīb, bi ḥurmati 'l-Fātiḥah.

And with Allāh is success. For the sake of the Beloved, for his sake we recite the opening chapter of Holy Qur'an.

Islamic Calendar and Holy Days

The Islamic calendar is lunar-based, with twelve months of 29 or 30 days. A lunar year is shorter than a solar year, so Muslim holy days cycle back in the Gregorian (Western) calendar. This is how Ramaḍān is celebrated at different times of the year, as the annual Islamic calendar is ten days shorter than the Gregorian calendar.

Four Islamic months are sacred: Muharram, Rajab, Dhūl-Qʿadah and Dhūl-Hijjah. Holy months include "God's Month" (Rajab), "Prophet's Month" (Shaʿbān) and the "Month of the People" (Ramaḍān), in which pious acts are rewarded more generously.

Months of the Islamic Calendar

1. Muḥarram
2. Safar
3. Rabīʿ ul-Awwal (Rabīʿ I)
4. Rabīʿ uth-Thāni (Rabīʿ II)
5. Jumāda al-Awwal (Jumādi I)
6. Jumāda uth-Thāni (Jumādi II)
7. Rajab
8. Shaʿbān
9. Ramaḍān
10. Shawwāl
11. Dhū'l-Qʿadah
12. Dhū'l-Hijjah

al-Hijrah

The 1st of Muharram marks the beginning of the Islamic New Year, chosen because it is the anniversary of Prophet Muḥammad's ﷺ historic *hijrah* (migration) from Mecca to Madinah, where he established the first, preeminent Muslim community in which he introduced unprecedented social reforms, including civil law, human and women's rights, religious tolerance, taxation to serve the community, and military ethics.

'Ashura

On 10 Muharram, ʿAshūra commemorates many sacred events, such as Noah's ark coming to rest, the birth of Abraham, and the building of the Kaʿbah in Mecca. ʿAshūra is a major holy day, marked with two days of fasting, on the 9th/10th or on 10th/11th based on a holy tradition (*hadīth*) of Sayyīdinā Muḥammad ﷺ.

Mawlid

Mawlid al-Nabī, 12 Rabiʿ al-Awwal, commemorates Prophet Muḥammad's birth in 570. *Mawlid* is celebrated globally throughout this month in huge communal gatherings in which a famous poem "*Qasīdah al-Burdah*" is recited, accompanied by drummers, illustrious poetry recitals, religious singing, eloquent sermons, gift giving, feasts, and feeding the poor. Most Muslim nations observe *Mawlid* as a national holiday.

Laylat al-Isra wal-Mi'raj

Literally, "the Night Journey and Ascension;" 27 Rajab is when Sayyīdinā Muḥammad ﷺ physically traveled from Mecca to Jerusalem, ascended in all the levels of Heaven from a rock in the Dome of the Rock, and returned to Mecca—while his bed was still warm. In the Night Journey, Islam's five daily prayers were ordained by God. Sayyīdinā Muḥammad ﷺ also prayed with Abraham, Moses, and Jesus in Jerusalem's al-Aqsa Mosque, signifying that Muslims, Christians, and Jews follow one god. This holy event designated Jerusalem as the third holiest site in Islam, after Mecca and Madinah.

Laylat al-Bara'ah

The "Night of Freedom from Fire" occurs on 15 Shaʿbān. On this night God's Mercy is great; hence, the night is spent reciting Holy Qur'an and special prayers, as well as visiting the deceased.

Ramadan

Many regard Ramaḍān, the 9th month of the Islamic calendar, the holiest month of the year. Muslims observe a strict fast and participate in pious activities such as charitable giving and peace making. It is a time of intense spiritual renewal for those who observe it. Fasting is meant to instill social awareness of the needy, and to promote gratitude for God's endless favors. The fast is typically broken in a communal setting, and hence Ramaḍān is a highly social month. At night, a special Ramaḍān prayer known as "*Tarawīh*" is offered in congregation, in which one-thirtieth of the Holy Qur'an is recited by the *imām* (prayer leader); thus the entire holy book of 6,000 verses is recited in this month.

Eid al-Fitr

"Festival of Fast-Breaking" marks the end of Ramaḍān and is celebrated the first three days of Shawwāl. It is a time for charity and celebration with family and friends for completing a month of blessings and joy. In the Last Days of Ramaḍān, each Muslim family gives "*Zakāt al-Fitr*"(charity of fast-breaking) which consists of cash and/or food, to help the poor. On the first early morning of *Eid*, Muslims observe a special congregational prayer, such as Christmas/Easter Mass or the High Holy Days. After *Eid* prayer is a time to visit family and friends, and give gifts and money (especially to children). Many specialty foods and sweets are prepared solely for *Eid* days. In most Muslim countries, the entire three days of *Eid* is a national holiday.

Yawm al-Arafat

"Day of ʿArafat," the 9th Dhul-Hijjah, occurs just before the celebration of *Eid* al-Adha. Pilgrims on Hajj assemble for the "standing" on the plain of ʿArafat, located outside Mecca, where they contemplate the Day of Standing (Resurrection Day). Muslims elsewhere in the world fast this day, and gather at a local mosque for prayers. Thus, those who cannot perform Hajj that year still honor the sacrifice of Abraham.

Eid al-Adha

The "Feast of Sacrifice," celebrated from the 10th-13th Dhul-Hijjah, marks Prophet Abraham's willingness to sacrifice his son Ismāʿīl on God's order. To honor this event, Muslims perform Hajj, the pilgrimage to Mecca that is incumbent on every mature Muslim once in their life if they have the means. Celebrations begin with an animal sacrifice to commemorate Sayyīdinā Abraham's sacrifice. In Islam, he is known as *Khalilullāh*, "God's friend." Many consider him the first Muslim and a premiere role model, for his obedience to God and willingness to sacrifice his only child without even questioning the command.

Glossary

ʿabd (pl. *ʿibād*): lit. slave; servant.
ʿAbdAllāh: Lit., "servant of God"
Abū Bakr aṣ-Ṣiddīq: the closest Companion of Prophet Muḥammad; the Prophet's father-in-law, who shared the *Hijrah* with him. After the Prophet's death, he was elected the first caliph (successor); known as one of the most saintly Companions.
Abū Yazīd/Bayāzīd Bistāmī: A great ninth century *walī* and a master of the Naqshbandi Golden Chain.
adab: good manners, proper etiquette.
adhān: call to prayer.
Ākhirah: the Hereafter; afterlife.
al-: Arabic definite article, "the".
ʿalāmīn: world; universes.
Alḥamdūlillāh: praise God.
ʿAlī ibn Abī Ṭālib: first cousin of Prophet Muḥammad, married to his daughter Fāṭimah; the fourth caliph.
alif: first letter of Arabic alphabet.
ʿAlīm, al-: the Knower, a divine attribute
Allāh: proper name for God in Arabic.
Allāhu Akbar: God is Greater.
ʿāmal: good deed (pl. *ʿamāl*).
amīr (pl., *umarā*): chief, leader, head of a nation or people.
anā: first person singular pronoun
anbīyā: prophets (sing. *nabī*).
ʿaql: intellect, reason; from the root *ʿaqila*: lit., "to fetter."
ʿArafah, ʿArafat: a plain near Mecca where pilgrims gather for the principal rite of Hajj.
ʿarif: knower, Gnostic; one who has reached spiritual knowledge of his Lord.
ʿĀrifūnʿ bil-Lāh: knowers of God.
Ar-Raḥīm: The Mercy-Giving, Merciful, Munificent, one of Allāh's ninety-nine Holy Names.
Ar-Raḥmān: The Most Merciful, Compassionate, Beneficent; the most repeated of Allāh's Holy Names.
ʿarsh, al-: the Divine Throne.
aṣl: root, origin, basis.
astāghfirullāh: lit. "I seek Allāh's forgiveness."
Awlīyāullāh: saints of Allāh (sing. *walī*).
āyah (pl. *ayāt*): a verse of the Holy Qur'an.
Āyat al-Kursī: "Verse of the Throne," a well-known supplication from the Qur'an (2:255).
ʿAzraʿīl: the Archangel of Death.
Badīʿ al-: The Innovator; a divine name.
Banī Ādam: Children of Adam; humanity.
Bayt al-Maqdis: the Sacred Mosque in Jerusalem, built at the site where Solomon's Temple was later erected.
Bayt al-Māʾmūr: much-frequented house; this refers to the Kaʿbah of the Heavens, which is the prototype of the Kaʿbah on Earth, circumambulated by the angels.
bayaʿ: pledge; in the context of this book, the pledge of initiation of a disciple (*murīd*) to a shaykh.
Bismillāhi'r-Raḥmāni'r-Raḥīm: "In the name of the All-Merciful, the All-Compassionate"; introductory verse to all chapters of the Qur'an, except the ninth.
Dajjāl: the False Messiah (Anti-Christ) will appear at the end-time of this

world, to deceive Mankind with false divinity.
dalālah: evidence.
dhāt: self / selfhood.
dhawq (pl. *adhwāq*): tasting; technical term referring to the experiential aspect of gnosis.
dhikr: remembrance, mention of God in His Holy Names or phrases of glorification.
ḍīyā: light.
Diwān al-Awlīyā: the nightly gathering of saints with Prophet Muḥammad in the spiritual realm.
du'ā: supplication.
dunyā: world; worldly life.
'Eid: festival; the two major celebrations of Islam are *'Eid* al-Fitr, after Ramaḍān; and *'Eid* al-Adha, the Festival of Sacrifice during the time of Hajj, which commemorates the sacrifice of Prophet Abraham.
farḍ: obligatory worship.
Fātiḥah: Sūratu 'l-Fātiḥah; the opening chapter of the Qur'an.
Ghafūr, al-: The Forgiver; one of the Holy Names of God.
ghawth: lit. "Helper"; the highest rank of all saints.
ghaybu' l-muṭlaq, al-: the Absolute Unknown; known only to God.
ghusl: full shower/bath obligated by a state of ritual impurity, performed before worship.
Grandshaykh: generally, a *walī* of great stature. In this text, refers to Mawlana 'AbdAllāh ad-Daghestāni (d. 1973), Mawlana Shaykh Nazim's master.
hā': the Arabic letter ه
ḥadīth Nabawī (pl., *aḥadīth*): prophetic *ḥadīth* whose meaning and linguistic expression are those of Prophet Muḥammad.
Ḥadīth Qudsī: divine saying whose meaning directly reflects the meaning God intended but whose linguistic expression is not divine speech as in the Qur'an.
ḥaḍr: present
Hajj: the sacred pilgrimage of Islam obligatory on every mature Muslim once in their life.
ḥalāl: permitted, lawful according to Islamic *Sharī'ah.*
ḥaqīqah, al-: reality of existence; ultimate truth.
ḥaqq: truth
Ḥaqq, al-: the Divine Reality, one of the 99 Divine Names.
ḥarām: forbidden, unlawful.
ḥasanāt: good deeds.
hāshā: God forbid.
ḥarf: (pl. *ḥurūf*) letter; Arabic root "edge."
Ḥawā: Eve.
ḥaywān: animal.
Hijrah: emigration.
ḥikmah: wisdom.
ḥujjah: proof.
hūwa: the pronoun "he,"made up of the Arabic letters *hā'* and *wāw.*
'ibādu 'l-Lāh: servants of God.
'ifrīt: a type of Jinn, huge and powerful.
iḥsān: doing good, "It is to worship God as though you see Him; for if you are not seeing Him, He sees you."
ikhlāṣ, al-: sincere devotion.
ilāh: (pl. *āliha*): idols or gods.
ilāhīyya: divinity.
ilhām: divine inspiration sent to *awlīyāullāh.*
'ilm: knowledge, science.
'ilmu 'l-awrāq: knowledge of papers.
'ilmu 'l-adhwāq: knowledge of taste.
'ilmu 'l-ḥurūf: science of letters.

ʿilmu ʿl-kalām: scholastic theology.
ʿilmun ladunnī: divinely inspired knowledge.
imān: faith, belief.
imām: leader of congregational prayer; an advanced scholar followed by a large community.
insān: humanity; pupil of the eye.
insānu ʿl-kāmil, al-: the Perfect Man, *i.e.*, Prophet Muḥammad.
irādatullāh: the Will of God.
irshād: spiritual guidance.
ism: name.
isma-Llāh: name of God.
isrāʿ: night journey; used here in reference to the night journey of Prophet Muḥammad.
Isrāʿfīl: Archangel Rafael, in charge of blowing the Final Trumpet.
jalāl: majesty.
jamāl: beauty.
jamaʿa: group, congregation.
Jannah: Paradise.
jihād: to struggle in God's Path.
Jibrīl: Gabriel, Archangel of revelation.
Jinn: a species of living beings created from fire, invisible to most humans. Jinn can be Muslims or non-Muslims.
Jumuʿah: Friday congregational prayer, held in a large mosque.
Kaʿbah: the first House of God, located in Mecca, Saudi Arabia to which pilgrimage is made and to which Muslims face in prayer.
kāfir: unbeliever.
Kalāmullāh al-Qadīm: lit., Allāh's Ancient Words, *viz.* the Holy Qur'an.
kalīmat at-tawḥīd: lā ilāha illa-Llāh: "There is no god but Al-Lah (the God)."
karāmat: miracles.
khalīfah: deputy.
Khāliq, al-: the Creator, one of 99 Divine Names.
khalq: Creation.
khāniqah: designated smaller place for worship other than a mosque; *zāwiyah.*
khuluq: conduct, manners.
Kirāmun Kātabīn: honored Scribe angels.
lā: no; not; not existent; the particle of negation.
lā ilāha illa-Llāh Muḥammadun Rasūlullāh: There is no deity except Allāh, Muḥammad is the Messenger of Allāh.
lām: Arabic letter ل.
al-Lawḥ al-Maḥfūẓ: the Preserved Tablets.
Laylat al-Isrāʿ wa'l-Miʿrāj: the Night Journey and Ascension of Prophet Muḥammad to Jerusalem and to the Seven Heavens.
Madīnātu ʿl-Munawwara: the Illuminated city; city of Prophet Muḥammad; Madinah.
mahr: dowry, given by the groom to the bride.
malakūt: divine kingdom.
Malik, al-: the Sovereign, a divine name.
Mālik: Archangel of Hell.
maqām: spiritual station; tomb of a prophet, messenger or saint.
maʿrifah: gnosis.
Māshā'Allāh: as Allāh Wills.
Mawlānā: lit. "Our master" or "our patron,"referring to an esteemed person.
maẓhar: place of disclosure.
miḥrāb: prayer niche.
Mikāʿīl: Michael, Archangel of rain.
mīzān: the scale that weighs our deeds on Judgment Day.
mīm: Arabic letter م.

minbar: pulpit.
Miracles: of saints, known as *karamāt*; of prophets, known as *muʿjizāt* (lit., "That which renders powerless or helpless").
miʿrāj: the ascension of Prophet Muḥammad from Jerusalem to the Seven Heavens.
Muḥammadun rasūlu 'l-Lāh: Muḥammad is the Messenger of God.
mulk, al-: the World of dominion.
Muʿmin, al-: Guardian of Faith, one of the 99 Names of God.
muʿmin: a believer.
munājāt: invocation to God in a very intimate form.
Munkir: one of the angels of the grave.
murīd: disciple, student, follower.
murshid: spiritual guide; *pir*.
mushāhadah: direct witnessing.
mushrik (pl. *mushrikūn*): idolater; polytheist.
muwwāḥid (pl. *muwāḥḥidūn*): those who affirm God's Oneness.
nabī: a prophet of God.
nāfs: lower self, ego.
Nakīr: the other angel of the grave (with Munkir).
nūr: light.
Nūḥ: the prophet Noah.
Nūr, an-: "The Source of Light"; a divine name.
Qādir, al-: "The Powerful"; a divine name.
qalam, al-: the Pen.
qiblah: direction, specifically, the direction faced by Muslims during prayer and other worship, towards the Sacred House in Mecca.
Quddūs, al-: "The Holy One"; a divine name.
qurb: nearness
quṭb (pl. *aqṭāb*): axis or pole. Among the poles are:
Quṭbu 'l-Bilād: Pole of the Lands.
Quṭbu 'l-Irshād: Pole of Guidance.
Quṭbu 'l-Aqṭāb: Pole of Poles.
Quṭbu 'l-Aʿdham: Highest Pole.
Quṭbu 'l-Mutaṣarrif: Pole of Affairs.
al-quṭbīyyatu 'l-kubrā: the highest station of poleship.
Rabb, ar-: the Lord.
Raḥīm, ar-: "The Most Compassionate"; a divine name.
Raḥmān, ar-: "The All-Merciful"; a divine name.
raḥmā: mercy.
rakaʿat: one full set of prescribed motions in prayer. Each prayer consists of a one or more *rakaʿats*.
Ramaḍān: the ninth month of the Islamic calendar; month of fasting.
Rasūl: a messenger of God.
Rasūlullāh: the Messenger of God, Muḥammad ﷺ.
Raʿūf, ar-: "The Most Kind"; a divine name.
Razzāq, ar-: "The Provider"; a divine name.
rawḥānīyyah: spirituality; spiritual essence of something.
Riḍwān: Archangel of Paradise.
rizq: provision; sustenance.
rūḥ: spirit. *Ar-Rūḥ* is the name of a great angel.
rukūʿ: bowing posture of the prayer.
ṣadaqah: voluntary charity.
Ṣaḥābah (sing., *ṣaḥābī*): Companions of the Prophet; the first Muslims.
ṣaḥīḥ: authentic; term certifying validity of a *ḥadīth* of the Prophet.
ṣāim: fasting person (pl. *ṣāimūn*)
sajda (pl. *sujūd*): prostration.
ṣalāt: ritual prayer, one of the five obligatory pillars of Islam. Also, to invoke blessing on the Prophet.

Ṣalāt an-Najāt: prayer of salvation, offered in the late hours of night.
ṣalawāt (sing. *ṣalāt*): invoking blessings and peace upon the Prophet.
salām: peace.
Salām, as-: "The Peaceful"; a divine name. *As-salāmu ʿalaykum:* "Peace be upon you," the Islamic greeting.
Ṣamad, aṣ-: Self-Sufficient, upon whom creatures depend.
ṣawm, ṣiyām: fasting.
sayyi'āt: bad deeds; sins.
sayyid: leader; also, a descendant of Prophet Muḥammad.
Sayyīdinā: our master (fem. *sayyidunā; sayyidatunā*: our mistress).
shahādah: lit. testimony; the testimony of Islamic faith: *lā ilāha illa ʾl-Lāh wa Muḥammadun rasūlu ʾl-Lāh*, "There is no god but Allāh, the One God, and Muḥammad is the Messenger of God."
Shah Naqshband: Muḥammad Bahauddin Shah Naqshband, a great eighth century walī, and the founder of the Naqshbandi Ṭarīqah.
shaykh: lit. "old Man," a religious guide, teacher; master of spiritual discipline.
shifāʿ: cure.
shirk: polytheism, idolatry, ascribing partners to God
ṣiffāt: attributes; term referring to Divine Attributes.
Silsilat adh-dhahabīyya: "Golden Chain"of spiritual authority in Islam
sohbet (Arabic, *suḥbah*): association: the assembly or discourse of a shaykh.
subḥānAllāh: glory be to God.
sulṭān/sulṭānah: ruler, monarch.
Sulṭān al-Awlīyā*:* lit., "King of the *awlīyā*; the highest-ranking saint.
Sūnnah: Practices of Prophet Muḥammad in actions and words; what he did, said, recommended, or approved of in his Companions.
sūrah: a chapter of the Qur'an; picture, image.
Sūratu ʾl-Ikhlāṣ: Chapter 114 of Holy Qur'an; the Chapter of Sincerity.
ṭabīb: doctor.
tābiʿīn: the Successors, one generation after the Prophet's Companions.
tafsīr: to explain, expound, explicate, or interpret; technical term for commentary or exegesis of the Holy Qur'an.
tajallī (pl. *tajallīyāt*): theophanies, God's self-disclosures, Divine Self-manifestation.
takbīr: lit. *"Allāhu Akbar,"*God is Great.
tarawīḥ: the special nightly prayers of Ramaḍān.
ṭarīqat/ṭarīqah: lit., way, road or path. An Islamic order or path of discipline and devotion under a guide or shaykh; Sufism.
taṣbīḥ: recitation glorifying or praising God.
tawāḍaʿ: humbleness.
ṭawāf: the rite of circumambulating the Kaʿbah while glorifying God during Hajj and ʿUmra.
tawḥīd: unity; universal or primordial Islam, submission to God, as the sole Master of destiny and ultimate Reality.
Tawrāt: Torah
tayammum: Alternate ritual ablution performed in the absence of water.
ʿubūdīyyah: state of worshipfulness. Servanthood
ʿulamā (sing. *ʿālim*): scholars.
ʿulūmu ʾl-awwalīna wa ʾl-ākhirīn: knowledge of the "Firsts"and the

"Lasts" refers to the knowledge God poured into the heart of Prophet Muḥammad during his ascension to the Divine Presence.

ʿulūm al-Islāmī: Islamic religious sciences.

Ummāh: faith community, nation.

ʿUmar ibn al-Khaṭṭāb: an eminent Companion of Prophet Muḥammad and second caliph of Islam.

ʿumra: the minor pilgrimage to Mecca, performed at any time of the year.

ʿUthmān ibn ʿAffān: eminent Companion of the Prophet; his son-in-law and third caliph of Islam, renowned for compiling the Qur'an.

walad: a child.

waladī: my child.

walāyah: proximity or closeness; sainthood.

walī (pl. *awlīyā*): saint, or "he who assists"; guarḍian; protector.

wasīlah: a means; holy station of Prophet Muḥammad as God's intermediary to grant supplications.

wāw: Arabic letter و

wujūd, al-: existence; "to find," "the act of finding," and "being found."

Yʿaqūb: Jacob; the prophet.

yamīn: the right hand; previously meant "oath."

Yawm al-ʿahdi waʾl-mīthāq: Day of Oath and Covenant, a heavenly event before this Life, when all souls of humanity were present to God, and He took from each the promise to accept His Sovereignty as Lord.

yawm al-qiyāmah: Day of Judgment.

Yūsuf: Joseph; the prophet.

zāwiyah: designated smaller place for worship other than a mosque; also *khāniqah*.

zīyāra: visitation to the grave of a prophet, a prophet's companion or a saint.

Other Publications available at www.isn1.net

Mawlana Shaykh Nazim Adil al-Haqqani

- Heavenly Showers (2012)
- The Sufilive Series (2010-2011)
- Breaths from Beyond the Curtain (2010)
- In the Eye of the Needle
- The Healing Power of Sufi Meditation
- The Path to Spiritual Excellence
- In the Mystic Footsteps of Saints (2 volumes)
- Liberating the Soul (6 volumes)

Shaykh Hisham Kabbani

- The Prohibition of Domestic Violence in Islam (2011)
- The Sufilive Series (2010-2011)
- Cyprus Summer Series (2 volumes)
- The Nine-fold Ascent
- Who Are the Guides?
- Illuminations
- Banquet for the Soul
- Symphony of Remembrance
- The Healing Power of Sufi Meditation
- In the Shadow of Saints
- Keys to the Divine Kingdom
- The Sufi Science of Self-Realization
- Universe Rising: the Approach of Armageddon?
- Pearls and Coral (2 volumes)
- Classical Islam and the Naqshbandi Sufi Tradition
- The Naqshbandi Sufi Way
- Encyclopedia of Islamic Doctrine (7 volumes)
- Angels Unveiled
- Encyclopedia of Muḥammad's Women Companions and the Traditions They Related

Hajjah Amina Adil

- Muḥammad: the Messenger of Islam
- The Light of Muḥammad
- Lore of Light / Links of Light
- My Little Lore of Light (3 volumes)

Hajjah Naziha Adil Kabbani

- Secrets of Heavenly Food (2009)
- Heavenly Foods (2010)